# NO COWARD

# The Harry Farr Story

By Janet Booth and James White

# Introduction

Harry Farr was born in north London in December 1890. His life ended while tied to a post, without a blindfold, shot to death by his fellow soldiers at the height of the First World War.

In between he served two years as a regular soldier before the war, fell in love, got married and became a father to baby Gertie, before spending two years on the Western Front with the West Yorkshire Regiment.

Yet his service to his country was to end in disgrace when he was officially branded a coward and condemned to death despite showing signs of shell-shock in what was to become the most infamous miscarriage of justice of the Great War.

For years his tragic demise was kept quiet by his relatives, the shame of the circumstances echoing down the generations until his granddaughter Janet Booth discovered his fate in the 1980s.

The shocking family secret, shared by Harry's wife Gertrude and confirmed by her mother Gertie, proved to be a catalyst for an extraordinary and ultimately successful campaign to pardon 306 British Empire soldiers who were executed for military offences in the First World War.

The Shot At Dawn campaign – led in parliament by Labour MP Andrew MacKinlay but supported by hundreds of relatives, volunteers and enthusiasts – took almost 15 years to come to fruition.

And it was Harry's case, taken by Gertie and Janet to the High Court, that proved to be the key to forcing a reluctant government and a hostile establishment into officially pardoning those who were executed for cowardice, desertion and throwing down of arms.

The recognition that the Armed Forces had acted erratically and at times illegally in the way cases were pursued and sentences handed down was a defining moment in the lives of Gertie and Janet.

As direct descendants of the unfortunate private they felt as if a cloud had been removed – and the hurt of the untimely death of a good and kindly man could finally be allowed to recede.

Here for the first time is the story of Harry's life, military service, trial and execution brought to life alongside the history of his descendants' fight for justice, featuring interviews with many key men and women in what was to be a drama played out in the national media.

He Was No Coward: The Harry Farr Story reveals the reality of what happens when ordinary people become part of something extraordinary – and how British history was changed forever.

## About the authors

Janet Booth is a retired secretary and the granddaughter of Private Harry Farr. She lives in Farnham, Surrey with her husband Jim to whom she has been married to for 53 years. They have two daughters and four grandchildren.

James White is a news and sports journalist, currently working as Deputy Sports Editor for MailOnline. He met Janet while working as a senior reporter for the Harrow Observer, a local newspaper in north-west London that campaigned with her.

## Authors' Note

During the early part of the pardons campaign, reference was often made to the 307 British and Empire soldiers who were executed for military offences.

This number was later established to be 306 and historian Julian Putkowski believes the 307 number was arrived at because of the original inclusion of a civilian in his book Shot At Dawn.

As a result, references made at the time to 307 soldiers have been corrected to 306 in this book, which is the total number of officers and men who were pardoned in 2006.

To document Harry Farr's time in the trenches of Belgium and France, the West Yorkshire Regiment's battalion diaries have been used to show how he moved in and out of the line, the casualties sustained and the appalling general conditions in the trenches.

References to his two battalions' activities during this period come from these diaries and are not continuously sourced throughout the text.

Quotes taken from newspaper articles are sourced but other quotes from key figures in this story are taken from interviews conducted by the authors and are consequently not cited in the notes on the text.

We are both extremely grateful to all those who spent time speaking about their experiences with regard to this campaign. Without their help this book would not have been possible.

**Janet Booth and James White**
**October 2017**

# Chapter One

Gertrude Harris, known as Gertie, was born nine months before the outbreak of the First World War, on October 29 1913, to Harry and Gertrude Farr. Theirs was a genuine love story, one that Gertrude would recall 80 years later with a moving sense of loss.

One of 13 children, of whom just nine survived into their teenage years, Gertrude senior grew up in cramped conditions in the family's rented rooms in Paddington, north-west London just off Harrow Road, near to where it meets Edgware Road. Having left school at the age of 14, Gertrude obtained a job as a scullery maid in the Jones household at one of the large houses of North Kensington. It was a white, narrow-fronted building with pillars on either side, with a small wrought iron balcony outside the first storey. The property was constructed on three floors, which included the basement and a small attic room at the top. There were several steps up to an imposing front door flanked by black wrought iron railings on either side. Gertrude would not have knocked on the front door on her first arrival at work but would have gone around to the side entrance where all the servants and trades people went. She recalled her first impression of the interior of the house as being beautifully furnished with expensive furniture and velvet drapes at the windows. It made her realise how small and shabby the rented rooms were where her parents lived.

She found it hard to comprehend that people lived in such splendid opulence. Never in her imagination had she visualised herself working in such a magnificent house. Her bedroom was to be the little attic room at the top of the house, which she shared with one of the other maids. Gertrude was thrilled to learn that she was to have her own bed because at home she had shared a bed with her sister and she remembered feeling quite excited at the thought of actually sleeping on her own.

Her little tin box of possessions had seen better days and was slightly battered and worse for wear. The box had been used by all her sisters when they had entered domestic service, then handed down to the younger siblings. It was just big enough to carry a spare set of clothes, underwear and nightclothes, a hairbrush and a few personal items.

She recalled feeling slightly nervous and apprehensive at meeting the lady of the house, but she need not have worried because she found Miss Jones to be a very pleasant lady. Although Miss Jones did make one stipulation about Gertrude's long hair; she must either get it cut or pin it up under her cap. The young woman opted for the latter suggestion.

It was while living here in the elegant St Charles Square with its handsome parade of Georgian townhouses that the young domestic servant first met Harry while walking to the park with her best friend Alice. She was just 16. Recalling him shortly before her death in 1993, in her mind she could still see a tall and handsome young man, a former soldier. She could visualise his good looks and talked lovingly about his beautiful grey-green eyes and his dark curly hair.

When relating the tale of how they met she had chuckled to herself that her friend Alice had 'fancied' Harry but he had chosen her. Harry bumped into the friends as they walked along Kensal Rise to the nearest park and Alice, who knew him, introduced the young man to Gertrude. Gertrude and Harry started 'walking out' together. They both loved visiting the Gaiety Theatre and many a happy evening was spent at the Hammersmith Empire watching the variety shows. The pair soon became girlfriend and boyfriend, and for the next four years they became inseparable, but not without some bumps in the road.

At the age of 20, Harry was four years Gertrude's senior, something her family were not happy about. She later told of the time when she was still employed by Miss Jones and of being 'rather naughty'. She said: 'He was four years older than me and I know my mother and my sisters, they all grumbled.

'They said at the time "he's too old for you, he's too many years older, you shouldn't have him".

'They grumbled at the time, that's how I remember it so well but I remember as we all say "I love him, I'm going with him and that's that".'[1]

So that she and Harry could spend a few precious moments together they devised a scheme where he would stand outside the house and give a whistle. Gertrude would pretend to the mistress or the cook that she had a letter to post and she would run down the road, still in her cap and apron, to meet Harry. Eventually Harry asked Gertrude to marry him and she said yes. He bought her a gold ring with a buckle engraved upon it, commonly known as a 'keeper ring'.

Unfortunately, her parents were not at all happy at hearing the news of their engagement – they thought him entirely unsuitable for her. They considered Harry to be too old and experienced for her, especially as he had served in the Army. She remembered saying to her mother 'I don't care what you say – I love him and that's that. I am going to be with him whatever your objections'.

Gertrude was very strong-willed and despite their disapproval she was determined to be with Harry. Just to prove that they were going to stay together Gertrude and Harry went along to the photographer's studio to have their photos taken for posterity. The photographs survive and they made for quite the portraits.

Harry stands resplendent in his Army uniform, his white gloves in one hand and a baton under his arm. His cap is placed on a side table proudly displaying the badge of the West Yorkshire Regiment, where he had previously served as a regular soldier.

Gertrude, aged 16, dressed in a beautiful white frilly blouse with 'leg of mutton' sleeves, which were voluminous and very fashionable at the time. Her smart serge skirt is teamed with a wide belt to accentuate her tiny waist and her long hair is swept up under a wide-brimmed hat, which is decorated with artificial flowers. On her delicate wrist she wears a large watch. They made a handsome couple.

Life couldn't have been more perfect for the pair and Gertrude started saving for her 'bottom drawer', where women would collect and store household items in preparation for marriage. Harry was earning good money working as a scaffolder on the building sites across London and Gertrude was still employed in the household of Miss Jones. They were able to put a few shillings by for when they eventually married.

It came as quite a shock in April 1913 when Gertrude realised she was pregnant - a child born out of wedlock would bring shame and disgrace on the immediate family. So what would her parents say? She hoped that when she told them they would not say 'I told you so' in reference to Harry.

Owing to the pending arrival of the baby they had to bring their wedding forward and were married as soon as possible. By the time of the wedding they had been together for three years and they were married in Kensington Registry office in the summer of 1913.

Being pregnant Gertrude had to leave the employment of Miss Jones, which meant there would be one less wage coming into the household. Nevertheless, they managed to rent a room in a tenement house in Wornington Road, North Kensington, and a baby, who was to be their only child, was born on October 29 of that year. They named her Gertrude Nellie, her middle name after Harry's sister who had emigrated to America, but the new baby would be known affectionately as little Gertie.

---

Henry Thomas Farr, who was known as Harry, was born to William and Alice Farr in North Kensington in 1890. He was their second son, William junior being the elder of the two boys. Nellie Christina, their sister, was the family's eldest child. Over the following years William and Alice had seven more sons, Sydney, Cecil, Charles, Fredrick, Edward, Stanley and Walter. In total the Farr family comprised nine boys and one girl.

William Farr senior had been a private in the Oxford and Bucks Light Infantry. In 1883 at the time of his marriage to Alice Grant he was stationed at Cowley Barracks in Oxfordshire. They were married in Oxford Registry Office. Alice was employed as a domestic servant by James Ramsey, an M.A. Tutor of Hertford College in the district of Headington, who was tasked with the spiritual wellbeing of parishioners.

On their marriage certificate it states that William was born in Birmingham where his father Joseph was a policeman. Alice was born in Evesham, Worcestershire, the daughter of Job Grant, a stonemason. The only photograph that exists of the couple shows Alice, a small pretty lady with dark hair seated with Nellie as a small child on her lap. William can be seen in his Army uniform standing tall and proud next to Alice.

After leaving the Army following 12 years' service, William was employed as a railway platelayer for the Great Western Railway. Wives would travel with their husbands and dwellings or railway cottages were built to house the families. Soon small communities sprang up along the vast rail networks between London and Wales. Nellie was born in Oxford, William junior is believed to have been born in Cardiff and the subsequent Farr boys were born in North Kensington, close to Paddington railway station.

Although no records survive, the Farr family home in Wornington Road, North Kensington would likely have been a few rented rooms in a tenement house. Family life at the turn of the century tended to be strict. William, with his military background and nine potentially unruly boys to keep in check, would probably have been a strict disciplinarian. For a family of the Farrs' social standing, food would have been basic and mealtimes strictly adhered to. Anyone misbehaving could expect to have had their knuckles rapped or their backside warmed with their father's leather belt.

Stanley was quite severely disabled. Little Gertie, as a young girl, remembers her uncle having to be pushed around on a bed on wheels upon which he would lay stretched out. She never understood what the problem was with Stanley but apparently he had always been 'poorly' since his earliest days.

Nellie left school at an early age and was employed as a domestic servant for a family in Shepherd's Bush. Fortunately this was not too far from the family home in North Kensington. When Nellie was about 19, the family for whom she worked decided they would emigrate to America. They asked Nellie if she would like to go with them to act as a nanny to their children. She asked her parents if they would let her go with the family. After a great deal of thought William and Alice agreed. Obviously they would miss Nellie but realised it was a wonderful opportunity for her to start a new life in a new country. But as a consequence they had to say goodbye to their only daughter with the prospect of never seeing her again. In fact Nellie never did see her parents again. She stayed in America, married and had a family of her own. When Nellie eventually return to England in the mid-1950s her parents had been dead for many years.

Perhaps inspired by his sister's boldness, Harry also chose an adventurous path and in 1908, when he had just turned 18, he decided to join the Army. He enlisted as a regular soldier in the First Battalion of the West Yorkshire Regiment, known as 'The Prince of Wales' Own' and whose motto was Ich Dien – I serve.[2] Naturally his father would have been delighted at Harry's career choice, being an ex-military man himself.

As a Londoner, it is a mystery as to why he joined a Yorkshire regiment, and little is known of his two years as a regular soldier. But later records showed he was considered to be a reliable and trustworthy soldier, with an exemplary record of good behaviour. The West Yorkshires had historical links with Buckinghamshire, the county which lies to the north-west of London, but was not known to recruit from there at the time of Harry's service.

The regiment's first battalion had fought in the Boer War until cessation of hostilities in 1902. By 1908 it was fighting again, this time in India 'against the Mohmand tribes on the North-West Frontier.'[3] Harry's movements during his two years in the Army are not known. It was after the end of his Army service that Harry met Gertie and their relationship began.

---

On August 4 1914, Great Britain declared war on Germany in response to its invasion of Belgium earlier that day. Britain was bound to protect Belgium by the Treaty of London, signed in 1839, yet was able to send just six divisions into Europe at the outbreak of war.[4] Consequently, all men who had recently served in the Armed Forces were still enlisted as reservists, and Harry was called up to the West Yorkshire Regiment, by telegram delivered to his home.

Most soldiers who had left the Army were automatically placed in the Section B reserve. It meant that for five years they could be called upon in the event of general mobilisation and were paid three shillings and six pence per week as a retainer, while also being obliged to undertake periodic training.[5] The West Yorkshire Regiment, with whom Harry had previously served, had a proud and storied history taking in the Napoleonic Wars, the Crimea and service in India and South Africa before its involvement in the First World War.

In a pamphlet entitled A Short History of The West Yorkshire Regiment, the excitable introduction to the unit nicknamed The Old and Bold claims: 'No regiment in the British Army has a more glorious history than The West Yorkshire Regiment (The Prince of Wales's Own), for its record and gallant and devoted service to King and country in many parts of the Empire is equalled by few and surpassed by none.'[6]

Indeed, so strong was the regiment's fighting tradition, its regimental march was *Ca Ira*, the French revolutionary song. In 1793 the regiment fought against French republican forces at the Battle of Farmars near the French frontier. After witnessing a frenzied French counter attack by soldiers singing *Ca Ira*, Colonel Doyle demanded his band strike up the same melody, saying 'Come along, my lads, let us break them to their own damn tune; drummers strike up the "Ca Ira".' The position was then carried by the Yorkshiremen 'at the point of bayonet'.[7]

Battle honours to add to those such as 'Namur 1695', 'Waterloo', 'Sevastapol' and 'South Africa 1899-1902' would include 'Neuve-Chapelle', 'Somme 1916, '18' and 'Ypres 1917, '18'. More than 13,000 names of officers and men were eventually added to the roll of honour held in the regimental chapel at York Minster, marking those who died on active service while a member of the regiment's 38 battalions.

Harry had previously served with the regiment's first battalion but its soldiers were already in France when he returned to duty, so he joined the second battalion. Before his passage to France, Harry was granted a weekend pass allowing him to return to London to spend a precious last few days with his wife and young child. Gertie's first birthday was celebrated that weekend and Gertrude promised to write to her husband frequently as well as sending him food and clothing parcels. After what must have been an extremely difficult farewell, Harry returned to camp having slightly overstayed his pass and subsequently being forced to forfeit four days' pay.

Family legend has it that Harry was pictured on the front page of a national newspaper, a photograph showing him and other troops eagerly awaiting the battle that lay ahead while billeted in tents on Salisbury Plain. While the photo has never been tracked down, the geographical claim makes sense because on November 4 1914, the Second Battalion, West Yorkshire Regiment, departed Hursley Park Camp near Winchester, Hampshire.
They marched to Southampton where four companies comprised 30 officers and 986 other ranks embarked the SS Mount Temple[8], a cargo ship with an intriguing history. In 1912 it was one of several ships to answer the distress call of the Titanic, but stopped short of assisting survivors because of the captain's concerns about thick ice, a decision that has remained controversial ever since. The ship was later to be captured and scuttled in the Atlantic by German sailors after a short battle on December 6 1916. Crew members were taken off before it was sunk with explosives, with its cargo of horses, food and newly discovered Canadian dinosaur fossils going to the bottom.

Like Harry the majority of his fellow comrades had never boarded a boat before - let alone left England's shores. Despite the reasonably smooth crossing to France, many of the men suffered from sea-sickness. Those not being sick were in good cheer and eager to face the enemy in battle. The general consensus of the men being that by Christmas 'this bloody war will be over'.

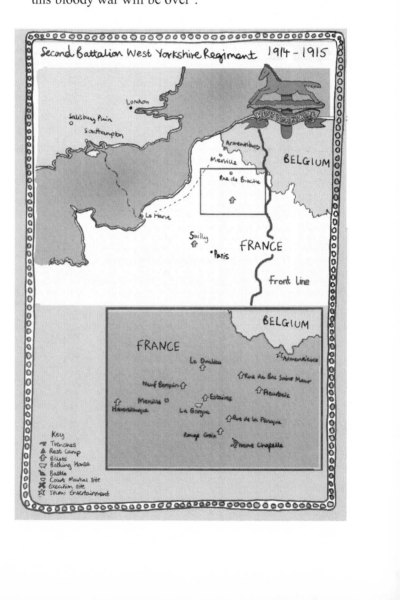

The soldiers arrived in France the following day, where they disembarked at Le Harve before marching to a holding camp. The Second Battalion, West Yorkshire Regiment was one of four regimental battalions that made up the 23rd Infantry Brigade of the British Army. The others were the Second Battalion, Middlesex Regiment; the Second Battalion, Scottish Rifles and the Second Battalion, Devonshire Regiment.

The 23rd was in the 8th Division, a regular British Army grouping formed at the beginning of the First World War, which in turn was a member of the 4th Corps and then the British First Army, whose commander was Douglas Haig when it was formed in late 1914.

From the holding camp, they entrained to Merville and then were billeted to houses and barns in the nearby village of Neuve Berquin. Within days they were ordered towards the lines and after just nine days of their arrival were sent into the trenches.

On November 13 at 11.30pm, the West Yorkshires relieved the Devon Regiment. The very next day the soldiers came under fire for the first time and suffered their first casualties, with three men wounded. No men were lost during this first stint at the Front, which was endured in wet and cold conditions. Indeed, one account of the battalion's first taste of trench warfare described the soldiers' 'great discomfort' in the heavy mud.[9]

Even at this early stage of the war, trenches were relatively well established with a system of lines running in parallel – the front, support and reserve trenches. The front trenches would contain fire trenches and command trenches with dugouts, support trenches would be up to 100 yards behind and have deeper dugouts. Reserve trenches would lie up to 500 yards further back and be even better protected. All three types were connected by communications trenches.[10]

The trench system meant that by November 1914 a stalemate situation had set in on the Western Front with 475 miles of fortifications extending from the North Sea at Nieuport in Belgium across France to the Swiss border via such areas that were to become iconic battlefields – the Somme region, Ypres, Vimy, Arras, Verdun and Metz. The front was to alter little geographically in the next 27 months.[11]

After their first stint, the men were quickly rotated out of the fire trenches and back to their billets where a pattern began of resting, training, followed by a return to the battlefield. As they left the line for the first time and marched to billets in Neuve Eglise, they were 'glad to leave the unsavoury trenches behind them'.[12]

At times during this period, the trenches occupied by the West Yorkshire Regiment soldiers 'were two to six feet deep in water, and cold mud baths were common; so also was the inevitable accompaniment – sickness'.[13]

On November 19, the battalion lost its first man to sniper fire, with another six wounded. For the next few days, in bitterly cold conditions amid falling snow, more men were lost to enemy action, more were wounded and the soldiers were shelled for the first time. Even when the men were resting in the barns and houses allocated to them behind the lines, there was no respite from the shelling, with the battalion receiving fire but luckily suffering no causalities or damage on November 23.

More rotations with the Second Battalion, Middlesex Regiment took place in trenches near Neuve Chapelle and the highlight of any action was a raiding party led by a Lieutenant Neave, who managed to blow up a house occupied by German snipers who had been targeting the British soldiers.

December began in the trenches with heavy shelling of the battalion headquarters after it occupied a sector in Pont Logy-Chapigny, north of Neuve Chapelle. Amid heavy rain, reinforcements arrived from Britain. The battalion's diarist noted that the communication trenches – the perpendicular connections between the support trenches and the front line – were 'in an awful state' even when compared with the generally poor conditions.

Across the British section of the front during this period, soldiers unused to their new conditions were suffering greatly as autumn turned to winter. Flanders in particular was known for its 'dampness' and trenches were frequently dipping below the water table.[14] For the soldiers, the 'trenches were always wet and often flooded several feet deep. Thigh-boots or waders were issued as standard articles of uniform… Pumps worked day and night to little effect'.[15]

The regiment's First Battalion was also in the line on the Western Front during this period, fighting with distinction during the Battle of Armentieres during a 17-day stint in the trenches, a scarcely believable period of time when compared with the usual three-day rotations.

Acting Sergeant Walter Watson recorded the difficulty of fighting in the rapidly deteriorating conditions. He wrote: 'The continual rain where the whole terrain had turned into a quagmire of liquid mud, making it difficult for the transport carrying supplies and weapons to continue along the muddy roads. Every so often they had to stop and push the vehicles over the cloying mud. Even more harrowing was trying to pull comrades out of the mud.

'Many men perished by slipping off the duckboards and disappearing into the slime. The days spent in wet and muddy trenches left some soldiers incapacitated by "trench foot" and invariably resulted in many of the men having a foot or both feet amputated. The pitiful sight of the horses and mules stuck in the rain sodden soil, struggling to free themselves from the mud.'[16]

The stints in the trenches were also getting longer, with the battalion spending six days at the Front before they were relieved, this time by men of the Devon Regiment. On December 14, 25 other ranks arrived at the front to increase the West Yorkshire's strength, despite there having been relatively few casualties.

During quiet spells, Harry was able to write letters home to Gertrude. He mainly answered her letters and thanked her for comfort parcels containing knitted socks and gloves and home-made bread pudding. She also sent him a mouth organ to play during lighter moments of rest away from the line.

On December 18, while in billets at an area known as Red Barn, the battalion's officers were called up for a 6.30am meeting with the brigadier at 23rd Brigade's headquarters. The West Yorkshire Regiment's colonel and captains were told that the Second Battalion, Devon Regiment would be attacking the German trench and two companies of Yorkshiremen would be sent in support to dig and make good any captured trenches. The battalion's other two companies would be held in reserve.

Fifteen minutes of shelling preceded the 4.15pm attack, the battalion's first of the war in what was later described as the 'prologue.to the Battle of Neuve Chapelle'.[17] It proved to be chaotic. The official battalion diary records: 'The Devon attack commenced from the left and was late in starting. The right company never advanced – thus creating a block in the trenches. The left company's attack was unsuccessful owing to the wire arrangements, but the left centre company occupied 150 yards of the main German trench.'

At midnight the entire Second Battalion of the West Yorkshire Regiment was ordered to take over the captured trench and improve it for defence, while their comrades dug in alongside. However, at 8am the Germans responded with hand grenades thrown 'in great quantities and very rapidly' forcing the men occupying the trench to retreat to the British front line.

As a consequence of this sudden action, the company of West Yorkshire soldiers attempting to dig on the right were left exposed and suffered withering enfilade fire. They also retreated, the attack ended in failure and the battalion suffered two officers killed, two wounded and 120 other ranks killed or wounded, almost all sustained in the retreat. Twenty-two Germans were taken prisoner and about 100 were killed in the attack.[18]

It is not known what role Harry played in the attack, but he almost certainly was a part of it. The battered West Yorkshires then spent the next couple of days in the trenches amid quiet conditions, finally being relieved by Second Battalion, Middlesex Regiment on December 21, before they made their way to billets. The battalion remained in the billets for three nights, resting and integrating a draft of 75 men to replace those killed and wounded in the previous action.

On Christmas Eve, the battalion was back in the line, relieving the Middlesex soldiers in the same trenches as before. The unofficial Christmas truce of 1914, in which gifts between opposing soldiers were reportedly exchanged, and spontaneous football matches taking place in No Man's Land, appears to have been observed by soldiers in the West Yorkshire's sector, although no record exists of meetings between the sides.

In the run-up to Christmas, little activity was recorded and on Christmas Day a sharp white frost made for dry conditions in the trenches. According to Everard Wyrall in The West Yorkshire Regiment in the War 1914-18, hardly a shot was fired and 'Christmas greetings were shouted both ways'. Wyrall also noted that an unofficial truce allowed both sides to recover and bury their dead.[19]

In the vicinity, the second Devons, whose men had been mauled just a week earlier during the attack on the German trench, which was supported by the West Yorkshires, found themselves moving into a sector where an unofficial truce was being observed. The battalion was tasked with relieving the second Cameronians on Christmas Eve night, and that unit had seen the German guns opposite fall silent during the day.

When it came to the relief, members of the Saxon regiment occupying the front line trenches were heard to shout 'a happy Christmas to you, Englishmen', and a brass band even played carols when the Devons took their places as the Scots left.[20] Sergeant William Williamson, of that unit, recorded that each side continued to 'play the game' and that Christmas Night was spent relatively peaceably, with just 24 rounds fired, and even then to harmlessly warn off a German drunk at their wire[21].

It was not until December 28, when the West Yorkshires were relieved, that some of the traditions of the season could be properly observed. The men were handed a decorative brass cigarette tin and tobacco from Princess Mary, together with a card wishing them a 'Happy Christmas and a Victorious New Year'. The gift was a one-off for British troops during the war and the tin and its contents were treasured by soldiers, so much so that Harry sent his home to Gertrude and baby Gertie.

Princess Mary, who was 17 in 1914, had wanted to provide soldiers and sailors with a gift, paying for it from her own allowance. However, when the scale and cost involved became apparent, a fund-raising effort was launched instead. Eventually 2.6m such tins were made for all Empire servicemen and the nurses in the field who cared for them – the standard issue containing 10oz of pipe tobacco, 20 cigarettes, a pipe and a tinder lighter for smokers and acid drops and a khaki writing case for those who did not smoke.[22]

The next day the battalion enjoyed a 'much-appreciated bath' at the divisional bath house in La Gorgue – the first they had taken in two months' active service.[23] But the following day was a sharp jolt back to the reality of the trenches in the wake of a torrential thunderstorm that turned the battlefield to a quagmire. Relieving the Middlesex regiment once again, the West Yorkshires discovered up to three feet of water in the support and communication trenches, with the front line firing trench also affected. The battalion diarist recorded that parapets were also falling in as a result of the rainfall.

New Year's Eve was cold and spent digging for many of the soldiers. After a consultation between the brigadier and members of the Royal Engineers, it was decided that a new trench was to be dug. In an action that neatly demonstrated the futility of the war the Yorkshires were in the middle of, the Allies were effectively retreating by building a new front line behind the flooded existing one.

Though just a matter of a couple of hundred yards behind and tactically more useful because it was to be sited on higher ground, in a situation where every foot and inch was fought over tooth and claw, it must have been a demoralising exercise to take part in. The division's mounted troops were tasked with the digging of the trench, 250 yards behind the support trenches of the battalion's centre companies.

The new year of 1915 began as the old one finished for the Yorkshiremen – cold, wet and in the trenches three-quarters of a mile north of the village of Neuve Chapelle. It proved a quiet day and two men were wounded. The next day the Second Battalion was relieved by the Middlesex regiment by 6pm and moved into billets in La Flinque, where it was held in the brigade reserve. There the soldiers remained for the next three days, when they were joined by a draft of 160 reinforcements.

On January 5 the battalion re-occupied its previous positions and again found the defences in a perilous state. To the left of their jurisdiction, a whole company-sized area of trenches has been 'given up'. Instead, the soldiers were forced to occupy breastworks – sandbagged and wooden walls constructed above ground to escape the flooding.

Such defences were vulnerable to attack by artillery because of their visibility and exposed position. According to A.J. Barker: 'These were more comfortable but also more vulnerable, and there was a sudden rise in the casualty rate.'[24] The weather remained inclement, with heavy rain persisting.

The next day, January 6, one man was killed and a lieutenant was taken to hospital. Two days later, on January 8, the West Yorkshires were once again relieved by the second Middlesex and headed to the divisional reserve, this time in billets in Pont Rirchon. One man was wounded.

The next two days were also spent in billets, where the companies took part in interior economy, which was the general maintenance of their sleeping areas, and spent time resting. The Commanding Officer, Lt Col G.F. Phillips was taken to hospital at Merville after the diarist had noted he was ill days earlier. Captain P.L. Ingpen took over command in his absence, and on the day the battalion returned to the trenches, January 11, another officer, this time a lieutenant named Cholmley, was taken to hospital. However, 63 rank and file soldiers arrived as the battalion went to the front, pushing it towards full strength as the men relieved their Middlesex counterparts.

Despite the hostile nature of the enemy just a few hundred yards in front of them, the battalion diary noted that the main cause of casualties was increasingly a result of sickness. Across the 23rd Infantry Brigade, the number of casualties suffered in the two months since its arrival was double the number of casualties from battle. The brigade evacuated 14 officers and 1,359 other ranks in the final two months of 1914, the Second Battalion, West Yorkshire Regiment accounted for five officers and 358 other ranks. Across the brigade during the same period, battle casualties were nine officers killed, 13 wounded and 553 other ranks killed, missing or wounded.[25]

For the Second Battalion, the harsh conditions in northern France were in strong contrast to its previous garrison in Malta from where it was recalled at the start of the war. According to A.J. Barker: 'Although battle casualties were initially light there was a steady loss of men due to the new ailments of "trench fever", "trench feet" and frostbite.'[26]

As well as via the ever-present water and mud, disease and sickness was carried by living sources, from the lice that infested every bit of clothing to the rats that feasted on the unburied dead. Paul Fussell writes: 'The stench of rotten flesh was over everything, hardly repressed by the chloride of lime sprinkled on particularly offensive sites. Dead horses and dead men – and parts of both – were sometimes not buried for months and often simply became an element of parapets and trench walls. You could smell the front line miles before you could see it.'[27]

Back in the trenches, the next two days were relatively quiet, although one man was killed and another wounded on January 12. One man was wounded on January 14, when the familiar pattern of relief by the Middlesex regiment was completed by 6pm, and the battalion went to the brigade reserve, staying in billets in La Flinque.

Three nights were spent there before a return to the same stretch of trenches, where two men were wounded. The next day, amid wet conditions, the diarist recorded that it was all quiet, but also that one soldier was killed and another wounded.

It is not hard to imagine the strain that the front-line troops were under. Despite no large-scale action, the constant deaths and injuries due to sniper and artillery fire in even the smallest section of the 440-mile-long Front[28] would have given an individual a sense of constant mortal danger. The drip-drip effect of these casualties would have been calamitous for morale as well.

On January 19, the trenches had dried out slightly, and four men were injured in action. On January 20, the battalion made its way to the billets in Pont Rirchon, again in the divisional reserve, and during their time away from the line, the battalion's officers and men were able to make use of the divisional bathhouse at La Gorge, amid fine weather. As the good weather continued, the West Yorkshires remained in billets, resting and taking part in interior economy.

Returning to the trenches on January 23, the company holding the right-hand section of the trenches found them very wet and instead occupied breastworks to the rear of the parados, the earth mound left originally to protect the soldiers' rear. On January 25, companies in the right and right-centre reported German activity in front of their lines and to the right at 8.30am. The ante was upped just over an hour later when a message was received from 8th Division, reporting that First Corps believed an attack was imminent and instructing recipients to be ready to fight 'at a moment's notice'. Rifle fire was recorded as being heavier than usual, but ultimately the expected attack never came, though three men were killed in the course of the day. The following day, it was off to the billets in La Flinque, this time in the brigade reserve. Two men were killed and one wounded, but a draft of 50 men arrived. On January 27, contact was made with the First Battalion at Stouplines.

The two battalions involved in the war at this stage were operating entirely independent of one another but shared a strong affinity, coming from the same regiment and for many of the soldiers, with the obvious exception of Harry, hailing from the same part of the world.

One man was wounded that day as the battalion remained in billets. The following day a sharp frost was recorded, and in the evening the relief of the Middlesex regiment was performed by 7pm. The diarist recorded more frost, a little snow and a 'brilliant moon', suggesting bitterly cold conditions for the men sleeping in dugouts, but also a lessened likelihood of night-time raids by the enemy. The battalions also occupied 'point d'appuis', leaving a section to act as garrison and repair it. The next day the cold conditions remained, with a hard frost but it was thankfully dry, and quiet. On the last day of the month, snow fell with water building in the trenches, but the enemy was quiet. The whole month of January had been spent either in the trenches or in nearby reserve, with no time spent any distance away from the guns.

On February 1, the battalion was relieved and went into the billets at Pont Rirchon in even colder weather. The next few days were also spent there, but on February 2 the battalion was struck by an undescribed tragedy, possibly shelling given that working parties were being formed, leaving two dead and two wounded.

On February 4, the officers were joined by Captains H.D. Harrington and J.A. Baff. Later that day, the battalion relieved Second Battalion, Middlesex Regiment in the same trenches, where they were to remain for three nights. During this time, four men were killed and five wounded, the majority of whom were hit during spells of German rifle fire and increased activity on February 5.

Two days later, the battalion was back in the reserve, for three nights, allowing rest and interior economy. By February 10, the battalion was back in the line, losing one man killed and two wounded on February 11. The relative lull continued for the next two days, with a man wounded on February 12 and relief the next day, when the battalion returned to Pont Rirchon billets for more rest and interior economy, enjoying baths on February 15 at the divisional bathhouse.

The following day saw a draft of 60 men arrive, led by a Captain F.P. Worsley. Among the men were a few from the regiment's Fourth Battalion. That evening the relief took place, with one man killed. Four men were wounded over the next three days and nights in the line, but generally it was recorded as being very quiet, with snow on the day of the relief.

Like clockwork, another three nights were spent in billets in La Flinque, with church parade on February 21, on the same day as Captain J.A. Barff was sent to hospital. The next day Captain P.I. Harkness and 30 men, most of whom were from the fourth battalion, arrived and impressed the diarist, who described them as a 'very good lot'.

The battalion then proceeded back to the trenches, where the next day Lieutenant E.W. Cummings was sent to hospital with diphtheria, the potentially fatal bacterial infection spread by coughs and sneezes or by sharing clothes or bedsheets used by a sufferer, all of which were likely in the close and filthy confines of trench life.

The next day 20 more men arrived, mostly from the fourth battalion, stemming the persistent dwindling of numbers that regular small numbers of casualties were causing. One man was killed, and another the following day, as well as two wounded. That night, February 25, saw the relief as normal and the battalion went to the Pont Rirchon billets. On February 26, Captain Ingpen, the acting commanding officer was sent to hospital and one man was wounded despite the relative lack of activity among the soldiers. For the first time that year, on February 27, the battalion resumed training, with companies undertaking route marches, physical activity and musketry. Orders were also received for the battalion to prepare to go for a rest, while the commanding officers were summoned to a conference with the brigade commander to discuss operations.

It was also announced that Lieutenant John F. Ruttledge was awarded the Military Cross for his actions on December 19 1914. The citation in the London Gazette later read, 'For great coolness and gallantry on 19th December 1914, near Neuve Chapelle. When his company were moving over open ground under very heavy fire, many casualties occurred and Lieutenant Ruttledge remained to the last, helping the wounded away to cover.'[29]

On the final day of the month, preparations were made for a movement to allow the battalion to rest and a church parade was held in the morning. Three working parties of 100 men were sent to dig new breastworks at 'B' lines, behind Rue Tilleroy, leaving three men wounded. However, all short leave for officers and NCOs was stopped, after 14 of them had enjoyed some time away. It would have suggested to the soldiers that something big was just around the corner.

## Chapter Two

The battalion left its billets at Pont Rirchon at noon on March 1, headed for Haverskerque for new billets where they arrived at 4pm in the grip of a snowstorm. The following day the billets were inspected by the commanding officer.

Unbeknown to the men and officers of the battalion, the British high command had settled on the area around the village of Neuve Chapelle for an intense offensive, in a bid to show allies and enemy alike that the British were a force to be reckoned with. The cabinet and Lord Kitchener, Secretary of State for War, 'authorised the British Expeditionary Force to attack at the Battle of Neuve Chapelle on March 10 1915, in part to show Joseph Joffre, the French commander-in chief, that it must be taken seriously.'[30] Tactically, the battle was to draw attention away from French plans elsewhere and if a breakthrough was achieved, it was to be followed by a fast push and capture of the strategically important town of Lille.[31]

On March 3, bathing was cancelled due to rain and the battalion's headquarters company moved to a new billet. A 'grenadier' or bomber company was formed for the purpose of throwing grenades during an attack on enemy trenches as preparation for the big attack intensified. A sergeant and eight men deemed not fit enough for the operations to follow were sent to Merville to work on road-making.

At 11am, all of the battalion's officer attended a conferences with the brigadier about the attack on Neuve Chapelle. They then visited an area known as 'B' lines in the evening to examine the ground where the battalion was due to attack. The following day the commanding officer, Captain Ingpen rejoined from hospital and assumed his temporary command of the battalion as companies carried out physical training and route marches in the morning in 'very cold and windy' weather conditions.

On March 5, the same pattern continued with training. The commanding officer also took the opportunity to survey the ground at 'B' lines, having missed the previous chance while in hospital. On March 6, company commanders led their men in training amid wet and cold weather and the following day a church parade was held, with a Roman Catholic service held at 9am and a Church of England one an hour later.

The battalion was ordered to be ready to head to billets closer to the front, and at 5.15pm it moved off, leading the brigade to accommodation in La Gorgue via Merville. An Indian convoy, made up of men who would give so much in the looming attack, held up the march by an hour. The battalion arrived at a factory where it was billeted at 9.30pm in cold and wet weather.

The next day, five men were injured, some severely, when they were hit by shrapnel in the morning. Two of the five died of their wounds later in the day. Despite being away from the firing line, shelling remained a terrifying occupational hazard. According to Paul Fussell, 'while being shelled the soldier ever harbored in a dugout and hoped for something other than a direct hit or made himself as small as possible in a funk-hole.'[32] Meanwhile, two platoons from A company were sent to La Basee Road as a digging party.

Officers were issued with a full set of orders on March 9 for the attack on Neuve Chapelle, and at 3pm further orders were received to march off in the evening. Details of the attack were explained to the men for the first time. The plan was to get Allied troops moving again after the entrenchment of the autumn before. There was also heavy pressure from London on the British commander in chief Sir John French to show the French high command the British fighting spirit.[33]

It was to involve two corps of British and Indian soldiers totalling 87,000 men from General Sir Douglas Haig's First Army and the attack was to take place along a front of just 2,000 yards near the village of Neuve Chapelle.[34] The village itself contained German machine gun posts set in houses, with multiple strong points on the approach.[35] Just before midnight the West Yorkshiremen marched out of their billets, to be held in the brigade reserve. At 1am on March 10, the battalion stopped for a hot meal on the road near La Flinque. At 5am it was held in an assembly area behind breastwork at Rue Tilleloy, in a line extending from brigade headquarters to point 13. A company was situated in a trench on the right of 'C' lines – it was in the line while the remaining four companies were held in reserve.[36]

At 7.30am the bombardment of enemy positions began, with wire-cutting shrapnel to aid any breakthroughs by the infantry. The first shell to fall was fired by an impressive 15" howitzer and weighed an incredible 1,400lbs. In forward positions across the front, troops attempted to shield their ears from the deafening barrage from 350 British artillery pieces – the biggest concentration of guns of the war by that stage.[37]

An hour later, the battalion moved into trenches known as point E that were vacated by the Second Battalion, Middlesex Regiment, which went over the top in the first wave of the attack. At 10am, the battalion joined the attack for the first time, with C and D companies under Captain Francis moving up to support the Second Battalion, Scottish Rifles at point 17-21.

At 11.30am, the rest of the battalion also joined the attack, with A and B companies under the commanding officer Captain Ingpen advancing to secure point 6 with the intention of working towards point 60. By 12.30pm those companies had occupied point 6, with one of the companies working towards points 60-83 and 60-61-8. However, their advance was blocked. At 2pm, the Worcester Regiment relieved the battalion's companies at point 6, and the Yorkshire Regiment, which took the line to the left.

The battalion then withdrew back to the British trenches and held the line 7-22 where it remained during the cold night that followed. Casualties had been severe, as they had across the front on the murderous first day of the battle. Twenty-three members of the battalion were dead including the adjutant, Captain R.A. Colwin. Fifty-one men had been wounded, and three were missing, but the savage fighting was to continue.

The 23rd brigade, whom Harry and the West Yorkshire Regiment soldiers were part of, suffered some of the worst losses of any Allied force during the action, which can be attributed to an artillery catastrophe of such proportions it would be difficult to imagine in a fictional farce. The 7th Artillery Brigade was brought to Flanders specifically for the attack and was allocated to the sector as early as February 26. However, it did not arrive in position until the afternoon of March 9 and the gunners were unable to set their howitzers up for their allocated targets. Because of the size of the barrage on the following day, it was impossible to re-adjust shots so the brigade's artillery attack was largely guesswork, which failed to make any impact on German defences.[38] This disastrous gunnery was compounded by a lack of high-explosive shells. Firing shrapnel at barbed wire tended to have little effect and in many places the wire was not cut.[39]

At 4am the next day, orders were received to move to point 41 and take over trenches held by the 25th Brigade. By 7am the battalion had relieved Royal Irish Regiment soldiers in trenches running from point 31 south west in front of chateau A, with one company in support on the road in Neuve Chappele. The intention was for this company to relieve the nearby Rifle Brigade when it moved, but the trenches were so full the relief did not take place. The battalion was reinforced with a draft of officers and men including the rejoining lieutenant Howsford and a new second-lieutenant, Sundins-Smith. The trenches were heavily shelled from 3pm and through the night. The losses that day were almost as severe as the first. Seventeen members of the regiment were killed outright – 16 men and the new officer Second-Lieutenant Sundins-Smith. Forty men and one officer, DSO holder Captain S. G. Francis, were wounded and four men were missing. The German resistance to the attack had increased dramatically on March 11 thanks to their ability to draft in troops quickly via train to the area of front most susceptible to being over-run. According to Stevenson: 'By day two at Neuve Chapelle the German number of defenders had risen from 4,000 to 20,000'.[40] Reinforcements included a fresh division, the 6th Bavarian Reserve among whose number was Adolf Hitler, a battalion runner.[41]

At first light – 5.30am on March 12, the Germans launched a local counter-attack at point A, held by B company. The enemy was repulsed 'at heavy loss to them', in no small part by the enfilade fire achieved by A company in trench 31 after trench 31-92 was captured from the Sherwood Forresters. It was retaken and the battalion diarist noted that 'very few of the enemy got back from this trench', in acknowledgment of the slaughter that occurred.

Again the shelling continued, inflicting heavy casualties on the severely depleted West Yorkshiremen, as they huddled in the trenches in cold and misty conditions. At 5.30pm orders were received to move with the Second Scottish Rifles under the command of the battalion's commanding officer, Captain Ingpen, to join up with Second Devon Regiment on the left and make a night attack, with the crossroads marked 'M.35. d.7.8' before continuing to the Pietre-La Russie road. At 10pm the battalion moved off, with the Scottish Rifles providing an advance guard. At 11.30pm the Scotsmen reported to the West Yorkshires that they had made contact with the Devon Regiment.

By this stage of the attack, the infantry soldiers were exhausted. Dead on their feet would have been an accurate description: 'The condition of the gallant fellows who had been fighting and marching to and from the trenches since the early hours of the 10th with practically no respite was by now pitiable. Men fell asleep at every halt, having to be roused by violent means.'[42]

Casualty numbers that day were less than the previous day but still overwhelmingly bad. Two officers were wounded, Captain A.H. Arnold and Captain G.H.G. Penny, the latter of whom appears to have survived the war. Alfred Huntris Arnold appears to have returned to the front and fought on but he died of wounds on December 30 1916 aged 24. His grave lies in East Sheen Cemetery in the London borough of Richmond.[43] Among the other ranks, 14 men were killed, 31 wounded and six were recorded as missing.

The end of the day formally marked the end of the battle when Lieutenant-General Sir Douglas Haig, commander of the First Army, issued an order for his soldiers telling them to turn advanced positions into defence ones. It also stated that no further advance would take place.[44] At 1am on the following day, March 13, the battalion lost touch with the Second Battalion, Scottish Rifles and stopped behind houses. Despite sending out patrols in a bid to regain contact, the action was unsuccessful, leading the battalion to return to Neuve Chapelle where it took up a temporary position on road 7-22 and stayed for the rest of the day. At 7pm the soldiers moved off and occupied a line of trenches from points 92-31. Grimly, the battalion diarist noted (we) 'found this trench unoccupied and full of dead.' During the evening the battalion also advanced as far as a cottage at point 92. The deaths and injuries continued for the battalion with two officers, Lieutenant H.O.B. Horsford and Second Lieutenant Kinnell, wounded. Both appear to have survived the war. Of the other ranks, four were killed, 28 wounded and three went missing during the day.

By 1am on March 14 the battalion's movement was complete, with two companies in the firing line and the other two in support. This was part of a wider relief of the 7th Division by Harry's 8th Division, the latter having sustained many more casualties and causing historian Geoff Bridger to remark: 'One would have thought they had already "done their bit"… the shattered 23 and 25 Brigades remained on duty!'[45]

Even under normal conditions it had been recognised that units needed to be rotated out of the line with regularity. On November 5 1914 Haig, who was to become commander-in-chief of the British Expeditionary Force the following year, wrote in his diary that 'my one thought was how soon I could get my battle-worn troops relieved and given a few days' rest out of the trenches and shell fire!'[46] Indeed on July 30 1915 he was even more explicit, saying: 'One lesson of this war was that troops could stand four days' hard fighting and then must be relieved.'[47] Of course circumstances such as this massed attack, which stalled within a day, prevented proper relief, but the consideration of the man who was to be Britain's most senior soldier for most of the war for the impact of front-line service on troops shows the incredible strain men such as Harry were under.

During a relatively quiet day after the horror of those which preceded it, there was little action with two men killed and one wounded. The battalion was relieved by the Second Battalion, Lincoln Regiment and marched to billets just a mile away from the battleground at Rouge Croix. Amid cold and misty conditions, a new draft of soldiers arrived to replace the killed and wounded. Finally, the soldiers of the battalion could rest, after four days of battle.

Despite some initial gains after a heavy bombardment, the Allies suffered heavy losses, with an estimated 3,500 dead and 8,533 reported as wounded.[48] Across the 8th Division, 218 officers and 4,387 other ranks were killed, wounded or posted as missing. For the West Yorkshire Regiment, the losses stood at two officers killed, five wounded as well as 55 other ranks killed, 162 wounded and 18 were posted as missing.[49] The Second Battalion had lost more than a quarter of its strength.[50]

This was despite the initial unprecedented bombardment and an estimated three million bullets fired by British and Indian soldiers.[51] The Germans lost more, without sustaining any kind of tactical defeat, with 16,000 soldiers killed or wounded during the defensive action.[52] In hindsight, no solace can even be taken from the improvement of strategy in future battles involving British troops. According to Bridger: 'The real tragedy is that many of the lessons learned at the battle were promptly discarded. For example, that vital element of surprise achieved by a short but very violent hurricane bombardment was not regularly used again for over two years'.[53]

However, the battle was judged as a partial success by the British 'because it restored the fighting reputation of their Army in French eyes'.[54] Some British officers saw the action as a success, because 'with a little better co-ordination and a little more refinement, they might well break through completely the next time.'[55]

The next day, March 15, in a bid to boost morale after the failed attack, Brigadier-General Reginald Pinney visited the battalion to bestow congratulations upon soldiers whom the commanding officer had recommended notice be made of their good work. Pinney was later to be immortalised in Siegfried Sassoon's 1917 poem The General about an affable yet incompetent leader:

*'Good-morning, good-morning!' the General said*
*When we met him last week on our way to the line.*
*Now the soldiers he smiled at are most of 'em dead,*
*And we're cursing his staff for incompetent swine.*
*'He's a cheery old card,' grunted Harry to Jack*
*As they slogged up to Arras with rifle and pack.*

*But he did for them both by his plan of attack.*[56]

The poem helped cement the view that common British soldiers were 'lions led by donkeys', a school of thought strengthened by historians in the 1960s and only recently challenged in new studies. Pinney was later promoted to major-general in charge of a division and survived the war, dying at the age of 79 in his native Dorset.

On March 16, the battalion relieved soldiers of the 25th Infantry Brigade in trenches in front of the old 'C' lines. It was a quiet day with occasional shelling and the West Yorkshires were reinforced with another draft of soldiers. In the evening of the following day, time was spent mending and improving the trenches. One man was killed and four wounded.

March 18 dawned cold and wet and despite the battalion diarist noting that it was quiet, three men were killed. Second-lieutenant Starington joined to bolster the depleted officer numbers and during the day the battalion headquarters was moved from the trenches to a point known as Home Farm. A quiet, snowy day followed and the battalion was relieved by the Second Battalion, Middlesex Regiment in the evening, moving to billets in Cameron Lane where on March 20 a draft arrived and an officer, Second Lieutenant Alexander, joined from the regiment's fourth battalion. Home Farm, the battalion headquarters, was hit by a shell and razed to the ground but there were no reported casualties.

More soldiers arrived the following day in another draft, including Major J.P. Barrington who was to take command and five more officers. The battalion moved to new billets in La Gorgue. This period of rest included another move, to billets in Bac St Maur the following day and on March 23 the separate companies took part in route marches, while 200 men were sent to the divisional baths. On the final full day of rest, more soldiers visited the bath house and officers visited the trenches in the evening. For the newly arrived officers apart from the commanding officer, this could have been their first taste of the front line.

On March 25 the battalion relieved the Third Battalion, Canadian Regiment in the trenches, completing the movement by 9.20pm in clear and frosty conditions with just one man wounded. The trenches were noted to be in good condition except for on the battalion's left side. The next three days were some of the quietest the battalion was to experience on the front, with three men wounded during the period spent in the trenches and no recorded fatalities. The weather continued in a similar vein – cold and fine with the ground drying. In front of them, no signs of movement were detected and the German trenches were noted to be 'very strongly wired'.

Indeed, across the front the contrast between the British and German trenches in terms of their condition, design and protection they afforded contrasted strongly.

According to Paul Fussell, 'the British trenches were wet, cold, smelly and thoroughly squalid. Compared with the precise and thorough German works they were decidedly amateur.'[57]

The reason for the stark differences has been attributed to the mindset of the opposing sides – the Germans were on enemy soil and after their initial 1914 gains, were happy to merely defensively occupy the ground they had won. As a consequence, they made themselves at home in bunkers that could be 30 feet under-ground, complete with bunk beds, electric lighting, kitchens and furniture.[58] For the British and their allies, the trenches were seen as a temporary solution before an attacking breakout.

In the trenches, the battalion was relieved by the Second Middlesex Regiment in the evening and marched to brigade reserve billets in Fleurbaix, suffering two men wounded. The time in billets was spent bathing at the brigade baths, with 30 men being sent there every half an hour. Despite a few shells falling near the billets, the regimental chaplain held a church service and officers visited from the First Battalion, West Yorkshire Regiment.

After the bathing was completed on March 31, the battalion rejoined the front line, relieving the Second Battalion, Middlesex Regiment after marching out of the billets at 7pm amid fine weather. The first day of April was spent in the trenches, and though noted to be a quiet day, one man was killed and another wounded. Two days later the battalion was relieved by the Middlesex Regiment and moved to billets in Fleurbaix amid rainy conditions. One man was killed and two more were wounded during the day.

April 4 was spent working for 100 of the men, with rain continuing all day. The next day the area was shelled, to little effect. But on April 6, a shell exploded in A company's billet, killing three and injuring eight. The soldiers fled the billets, taking shelter in dugouts and even fields nearby. As a result, the whole battalion moved to new billets in Rue de Biache. The next day the West Yorkshires moved again, this time marching to billets one mile from Sailly, where they were held in the divisional reserve. The next two days were spent training and involved route marches.

On April 10, the companies were placed under the control of the commanding officer's company, amid fine weather. The officers received a visit from a captain from the First Battalion, West Yorkshire Regiment, which was stationed at nearby Houplines, meaning 'constant visits were possible between the two'. Junior officers who volunteered also received riding instruction. The next day this seemingly idyllic period continued in fine weather, with an open-air Church of England service in the afternoon.

The battalion marched back to Fleurbaix and into the brigade reserve on April 12. On the way, the battalion was inspected by the commander-in-chief, Field Marshal John French, amid fine weather. The purpose was to congratulate the officers and men for the part they played in the Battle of Neuve Chapelle.[59] The next day officers from the battalion were sent to visit the second line defence posts. On April 14, some of them visited new trenches currently occupied by the second battalion of the Devonshire Regiment. As a fellow member of the 23rd Infantry Brigade, it was likely the West Yorkshire Regiment would soon be rotating into those same trenches. The battalion diary also noted that two territorial battalions had been attached to the brigade, an indication that an attack could be in the offing.

Training continued the next day, with revolver practice and a route march in fine conditions. On April 16, fatigue duty was carried out in ditches in the area, before 100 men of B company were sent in motor lorries to the IV Division 'Follies' in Armentieres. The Follies were a dance troupe that were performing to crowded houses, a forerunner of similar attractions that proved a hit with soldiers across the Army because they helped 'to dissipate the awful stress of life in the trenches'.[60]

Recreational activities were important for British troops, however tired they were. According to Stevenson: 'Games – and especially football – were the most immediate form of recreation for even exhausted British troops when they left the line, supplemented by canteens, cafes, clubs such as the "Toc H" refuge at Poperinghe, and concert parties, thus linking in with Edwardian England's music-hall enthusiasms and sporting obsessions.'[61]

The following day, after route marches, more men were sent to watch the show, 100 from A company and the same number from D company. The fine weather meant the ground was hardening and would be suitable for riding, the diary noted somewhat incongruously. The next day, April 18, church parades were held after a service. Then the battalion returned to the trenches for the first time in more than two weeks.

The Devonshire Regiment soldiers were relieved, and the West Yorkshiremen were joined by officers and NCOs from battalions of the West Riding Regiment, who were there for instruction. Soldiers from that regiment also visited for 24-hour periods to learn about fighting on the front line. During the spell in the trenches, the author of the diary noted that the trenches were very good, 'dry and safe' with a good water supply. B Company was held in reserve during this period, which coincided with a period of fine weather and little enemy activity.

At a conference on April 20, the brigadier told battalion commanding officers he had postponed offensive operations. At the conference the senior officers also visited trenches and studied the ground in the direction of Fromelles. The following day was quiet and pioneers worked on the HQ farm, which was noted to be fairly comfortable. Just one man was wounded on a fine day weather-wise, the first such casualty in a while.

On April 22, the remains of the Ancienne Abbaye de Chartreux was shelled again, but with little effect. Two were killed and one wounded during the day, leading to a burial service in the grounds of the Abbaye at 10pm. Ominously, the regimental diarist noted that the following day, a build-up of batteries had begun in the neighbourhood and as a consequence, German artillery had been 'searching the ground behind HQ.' It was announced that Captain H.D. Harrington had been awarded a DSO.

The following day, the battalion was relieved by the first battalion of the Worcester Regiment and moved out of the trenches in the evening. Before they moved, they heard heavy artillery and rifle fire towards Rue du Bois. After relief, the battalion marched to billets to the north-west of Sailly, arriving at 1am the following morning.

The next few days were dedicated to rest and training. On April 26, the only activity of note was a voluntary Church of England service in the morning. A couple of days later, the battalion marched to billets in Doulieu, two miles further north. There, a huge draft of men led by a single officer, Lieutenant Sharpe, arrived. In total the battalion was reinforced by 247 other ranks, meaning an approximate 30 per cent increase in strength, and another sign that an attack would soon be made.

On April 28, the battalion was involved in brigade-wide training during which it advanced in artillery formation over fields, perhaps to imitate a creeping barrage. The next couple of days were spent partaking in physical training and in command of their commanding officer's company. On May 1 the brigade, at Doulieu, six miles west of Armentieres, was ordered to be ready at short notice. The soldiers were told by their officers that blankets were to be left behind and great coats were placed on wagons, a sign that would have been seen by some that an attack was imminent. But at 10.30am the battalion carried out a tactical exercise in fine and warm weather.

The next day the battalion marched to Estaires, a mile or so south of their position where they enjoyed 'very good' billets. After rain fell during the day, men were provided for two digging parties in the evening, leaving a man wounded. The West Yorkshires spend another night in the relatively luxurious billets on May 3 despite receiving orders to move, which were then cancelled. However, they were ordered to march to 'very bad and very crowded' billets south of Sailly the next day, and spent their time looking for accommodation as a consequence of being outside of their area. A second-lieutenant, called Gabriel, was sent to hospital and by May 5 billets were found for A, B and headquarters companies at Rue du Quesnoy. The next day working parties were required to dig assault trenches, another sign a big attack was imminent, to both the British soldiers and the enemy. One man was injured during the day and on May 7, detailed orders reached company commander level, when they attended a conference at battalion headquarters. That evening at 6pm just an hour before marching off, rain caused the postponement of the operations for 24 hours. Even so, the men were issued with gas masks and respirators in preparation for enemy counter-attacks. The next day proved to be an anti-climatic lull, because preparations had already been made.

The weather was fine and in the evening, following a short speech by the colonel, the Yorkshiremen marched to their positions in 'J' assembly trenches, with just haversacks, a ground sheet or oil sheet as it was then known but without their great coats. Second-Lieutenant Gabriel rejoined the battalion from the hospital, just in time for the attack. The Second Battalion was being held in reserve for what was to be known as the Battle of Aubers Ridge.[62] The attack was designed to assist a French operation north of Arras, with commander-in-chief Joffre targeting the German-held Vimy Ridge.[63] At 5am on May 9, the artillery bombardment of the enemy's trenches began, with the attack launched just 40 minutes later.

The 23rd Infantry Brigade, which included the Second Battalion, was held in the divisional reserve. At 6.30am, the battalion made its way from J to E trenches, just 500 yards from the firing line, where it remained all day but the planned night attack for later that day was subsequently cancelled. During the shelling and small arms fire from the Germans, Lieutenant R.J. Legad was wounded in the head and died of his wounds. Two other ranks were killed, 13 were wounded and three were posted as missing.

The following day shortly after midnight, the companies received an order to return immediately to F trenches but again received an order cancelling the move just 15 minutes later. The battalion diary recorded: 'There was a constant rifle fire and general agitation all night but the regiment had a little sleep.' It was no wonder the soldiers could not sleep under such conditions, many had been awake for more than 24 hours and some for as long as two days if they had drawn sentry duty on the night before the attack.

The German forces attempted a 'half-hearted' counter attack at dawn, but it was not a success. The weather was fine and warm that day, and at about 1pm the battalion left the trenches for a temporary bivouac. But by 8pm that night, the soldiers were back in the line, occupying F trenches again which the officer commanding remarked were good trenches apart from a salient occupied by B company, which was very close to the enemy's trenches. Throughout the night, that company came under fire from the German who targeted the area with trench mortars, but led by Lieutenant Cherry, the men were able to return fire with mortars of their own. One man was killed and two wounded during the day and the following day was quiet. The French attack on Vimy Ridge failed after a week, costing the French 100,000 casualties. The British attack on Aubers Ridge 'failed ignominiously'.[64]

By this time Harry had been withdrawn from the front line, suffering from what was becoming known as shell-shock when he was taken off duty on May 9. Details of his movements are unknown, but it is likely he would have arrived first at a casualty clearing station located in support trenches or nearby, before being sent back to a base hospital run by the Royal Army Medical Corp.

There is no evidence he returned to Britain, although soldiers with severe cases of shell-shock were often treated back at home. These were located further away from the front yet not necessarily out of earshot of the guns. Many British hospitals were located on the coast in places such as Le Touquet, Boulogne and Calais.

Since the beginning of the war, soldiers engaged in front line duties had presented to aid stations and hospitals with symptoms such as blurred vision, memory loss, spasms and trembling hands.[65] By 1915 the term shell-shock was in common parlance. However, rather than being viewed as psychological condition, some doctors and researchers were viewing the symptoms more in line with a neurological disorder or the result of a concussion from a shell blast.

Treatment for the condition largely involved rest away from the front line and possibly some talking therapies that we would now refer to as counselling. However, despite this chance to rest and recuperate away from the danger, fear and alarm of the front, treatment of nerve cases was in its early infancy. In extreme circumstances, some doctors utilised electric shock therapy and isolation therapy on sufferers, but both were unproven and experimental.[66] Stevenson said: 'Post-traumatic stress disorder... was exacerbated by the special conditions of static warfare in which soldiers endured repeated bombardments in confined spaces with little control over their fate, and lived day by day in close proximity to their comrades' decomposing remains.'[67]

Yet even if the condition was receiving recognition, sensitivity and experience in treating it among doctors and psychiatrists were lagging behind. Even today, some historians suggest that shell-shock – or combat stress as we would now call it – was easily faked. Corrigan writes: 'The difficulty, as with gas injuries, was that "shell-shock" was easier to fake than a physical wound, and was a defence often seized upon by offenders with no other excuse for their behaviour.'[68] Harry could have expected to be treated with a combination of rest and counselling among other techniques. And they were reasonably successful. Eighty-seven per cent of Britain's 80,000 recorded cases of shell-shock saw the soldier return to the front within a month.[69]

For Harry, a return to fighting condition would take some time longer.

## Chapter Three

In the summer of 1915, Gertrude received a letter from France but she did not recognise the handwriting on the envelope as Harry's. The letter stated that Harry was ill in hospital. He had been evacuated from the Houplines area in May as he had been suffering from what was known as shell-shock. Stricken by nervous exhaustion, his hands had been shaking too much to hold a pencil so a nurse at the hospital had written the letter for him. It was to be the last letter from Harry that Gertrude received.

After the extended period behind the lines, Harry was assessed and certified fit. He was sent back to the West Yorkshire Regiment, this time joining the First Battalion, part of the 18th Infantry Brigade, 6th Division in October 1915.

The First Battalion had seen action since the beginning of the war, arriving in France at St Nazaire in early September 1914 and taking part in the Battle of the Aisne later that month as both sides fought to reach the sea and outflank one another. The following year the battalion took part in the Second Battle of Ypres at Hooge, Belgium, where German forces used flamethrowers for the first time. In late 1915 the brigade was located in the Ypres salient, Belgium, the scene of five major battles throughout the war.

On October 21, 89 men including Harry joined the battalion while it was in camp behind the line.[70] Shortly after, the Germans launched a huge barrage against Allied rest areas including Poperinghe and all along the front in retaliation for Royal Artillery shelling of their own billets. Although little damage was done, the sound of the guns which had caused Harry to fall ill before had begun all over again for him.

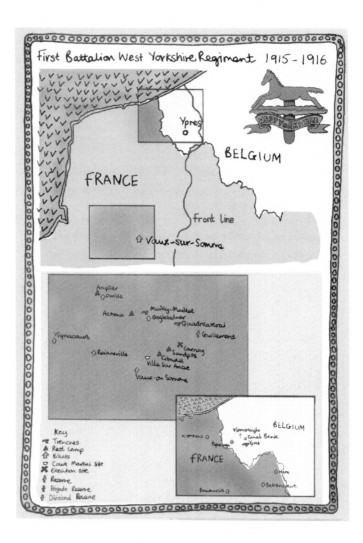

First Battalion West Yorkshire Regiment 1915 - 1916

Ypres

BELGIUM

FRANCE

Front line

⚑ Vaux-sur-Somme

Amplier
○ Orville
Acheux △   ⚑ Mailly-Maillet
           ○ Englebelmer
              ⚑ Quadrilateral
                   ⚑ Guillemont
Vignacourt
⚑
                  ✗ Carnoy
   ○ Rainneville    △ Sandpits
                    ○ Citadel
                    Ville-sur-Ancre
              Vaux-on-Somme

Key
⚑ Trenches
△ Rest Camp
⚑ Billets
▽ Court Martial site
✗ Execution site
⚑ Reserve
⚑ Brigade Reserve
⚑ Divisional Reserve

BELGIUM
Vlamertinghe
Wormhout        ↑ Canal Bank
      Poperinghe   ⚑ Ypres
FRANCE
                        Otem
                    ○ Sebrancourt
   Boucmaisil ○

Later in October, the brigade assembled a composite force to parade before King George V who was visiting. Two officers and 20 other ranks of the West Yorkshires were sent along. A telegram was later sent on behalf of the monarch, which read: 'He was very pleased with the soldierly bearing of his troops.'

At the end of the month the battalion began an 11-day spell in the trenches, characterised by heavy rain, collapsing fortifications and mud. By November 3, an officer had been killed, and almost all dugouts had collapsed, leaving the men with little respite from the appalling weather. Officers estimated the damage done to the trench system would take months to repair, stating that 'every effort was made to contend with the water' during one period of three days and nights of continuous rain.

In mid-November, the soldiers held trenches in the Ypres salient and although mostly quiet, endured some shelling. At the end of their stint, a weary-sounding entry in the battalion's diary stated: 'The 6th Division has at last started its long promised rest away from the sound of gun and rifle fire. It has been out in France since 10th September 1914 and first come under fire on 19th September 1914. Since that date, except for the move from The Asine to Hazebrouck and the move from Armentieres to Ypres, it has never been out of gun fire and has taken its turn in the trenches for over a year. The battalion has been with VI Division for the whole of this period.'

The following 15 days were spent in billets in Houterkerque, where the battalion rested and took part in the usual drills and training exercises. It was also a chance to refit, with the soldiers replacing damaged and worn equipment and weapons. On December 5, the battalion marched to Elveringhe, spending the next 10 days forming working parties to carry out tasks such as repairing paths. Despite not being in the line, casualties were sustained when the parties were shelled and fired upon by riflemen.

After another short break and a chance for a bath, the battalion returned to the trenches on December 15, bussed into their sector in Ypres. Working parties at night continued, with a few men injured at times, but the little happened until December 19 when the area came under artillery bombardment and that frightening phenomena of battle, the use of gas.

The action began at 5.30am when the British-held trenches came under heavy rifle fire. Then at 6.45am, when troops were stood to in anticipation of an attack, shells containing gas were fired by the Germans. The use of chemical weapons by either side was nothing new, with the first Western Front attacks taking place earlier in the year. However, this attack was the first time that German troops had used a combination of chlorine and phosgene gases. Chlorine was a proven killer but required high levels of inhalation to ensure fatalities. Gas masks, issued to all troops, were proving increasingly effective against its use. Phosgene was even deadlier, but its density meant it was harder to spread and because symptoms were not manifested until 24 hours later, not immediately effective in incapacitating defenders. Mixed with chlorine, it proved easier to spread and the combination was immediately effective, aiding the troops as they advanced through No Man's Land. In this instance, no attack came against the First West Yorkshires, but the effect of the gas was instantaneous, and horrifying. During the day, 11 men died and 23 were wounded, two suffering the effects of gas. Total Allied losses on the day as a direct result of gas were 1,069 casualties and 69 deaths.

The following day the battalion relieved the Durham Light Infantry amid heavy shelling by the Germans, but thankfully most of it was directed at other targets, save a few 'whizz bangs' – shells that travelled faster than the speed of sound which gave disconcertingly little warning to soldiers. They were named because troops would hear the whizz of the shell before the bang of the guns. One man was killed during the day, three wounded and four transport horses also lost their lives.

The run-up to Christmas was characterised by wetter weather and the front was consequently quiet. The battalion was able to work on its trenches, draining them and improving damaged parapets. Harry's second Christmas in France saw the battalion away from the front after it was relieved of front-line duties on Christmas Eve afternoon. Men were given the chance to bathe, handed a free issue of beer and plum puddings and received a visit from the commanding officer. The battalion diarist noted that the soldiers were 'very happy and pleased to be out of the trenches on Xmas Day'.

Shortly after Christmas the brigade formed a machine gun company, in line with infantry regiments across the British Army. One lieutenant and 37 men transferred to this company, although it is not known if Harry was among them. Their new role was to maintain, load, re-arm and fire the Vickers gun, a weapon that required skill from its operators to prevent overheating during firing. Those still in traditional infantry companies were required to continue training away from the front, including short route marches and gas mask or 'tube helmet' practice.

The battalion was back in the trenches for the end of the year and the start of the new one. On December 30, the battalion's headquarters was shelled out of Potinze Wood, suffering two men killed and four injured. Despite being the target of 'whiz bangs' on New Year's Eve, that day and the following one the action was light and no casualties were suffered. The pattern of 'useful' patrols into No Man's Land and shelling continued until the Durham Light Infantry relieved the men, who swapped the danger of the front line for the drudgery of nightly working parties.

This pattern of rotation in and out of the front where aggressive patrolling was a key strategy was replicated across the British Army. According to Judge Anthony Babington, units in the line were required to take part in limited attacks, night raids and sniper fire to gain control of No Man's Land. He wrote: 'This policy frequently evoked a retaliatory effort by the enemy and it accounted for an average of about 35,000 British casualties a month… When units were relieved from the line they were sent to reserve or to rest areas, where to the irritation of both the junior officers and the men the bulk of their time was occupied in drill parades, training and inspections.'[71]

Conditions during the winter were particularly grim. According to Everard Wyrall: 'The maintenance and repair of the defences amidst all the discomfort of winter went on without cessation. The inclement weather brought the floods and these, combined with the enemy's shells and bombs, destroyed trenches and dug-outs and communications and all such damage had to be constantly made good promptly under fire and almost entirely at night.'

Other stresses endured included constant shelling, sniper fire at any time and patrols in No Man's Land, which would often lead to contact with the enemy and bombing fights. 'Mining and counter-mining with its consequent heavy strain on the nerves went on unceasingly.'[72]

On January 7 the battalion diarist noted a number of officers and men were mentioned in despatches on January 1. Of particular interest was the mention of Sergeant J.W. Booth, who was later to give evidence against Harry at his court martial, by that time as Quarter Master.

On its return to the trenches the battalion endured sporadic shelling and at one point the parapet collapsed in 'one or two places', but casualties were light. This pattern continued for the rest of January, although in its next spell in the trenches the battalion came under heavy sniper fire, which led to the loss of one man and others injured, including the battalion adjutant T.H.W. Armitage.

Returning to the trenches at the beginning of February, the battalion encountered a spell of brighter weather, and as a consequence artillerymen on both sides took the opportunity to open up on the trenches in front of them, but casualties among the Yorkshires were light. After a spell in billets, the battalion returned to the same trenches that they had exited days earlier. On February 11, artillery was noted to be 'exceptionally active, killing one man and injuring five more'.

More than 100 miles away in Verdun, France, the Germans were set to launch their biggest offensive of the year, yet it was cancelled by bad weather. The French soldiers opposite them in an eight-mile stretch of the front would face one of the biggest bombardments of the war, but in the days preceding the February 21 attack, forces opposing the Germans were to face attacks across the Western Front.

The following day artillery fire continued, preceding an attack by the Germans on the XIV Division and the French troops about three to four miles north of Potijze at 2.30pm. Artillery fire on the sector continued throughout the day and well into the night, leaving three dead and six injured. The next day, the bombardment continued, targeting an area known as Railway Wood for two-and-a-half hours in the morning. Although no men were killed, 23 were injured. On February 14, German artillery shells fell again on the battalion and Railway Wood came in for more sustained fire, killing five and injuring 15.

By the time the first battalion left the trenches the next evening, it had suffered losses of nine killed, and 51 hurt. This casualty rate – about six per cent of battalion strength in just one five-day spell in the trenches – is particularly high for ordinary front-line duties. But it underscores the losses suffered by the British Army during the First World War, when 7,000 soldiers were killed and wounded every day 'as a matter of course'.[73]

Of course there was no let-up to the routine and despite being stationed in billets, officers and men were required to make up working and carrying parties each day. Back in the trenches and after a bright first full day, freezing conditions set in, with snow falling for almost all of the second day, and despite the battalion diarist noting that it was quiet, one soldier was killed and five wounded. However, a patrol with bombing party attached was made across to the German wire, returning with 'useful' information. Snow continued the next day, but enemy activity fell away and the following day the battalion was relieved.

In March, the battalion started its next spell in the trenches and on the second day at 4.32am, troops and Lewis gunners on the front line opened up for 10 minutes in a bid to attract attention away from an Allied attack on an area known as The Bluff. The Bluff was a mound made of canal-building spoil situated south of Ypres, providing some of the best views of the salient. The Germans retaliated by directing shells on the West Yorkshire's positions and heavy gunfire was traded for the rest of the day and the night, yet no-one was hurt or killed. The attack on The Bluff was a strategic success for the British Army, which captured it despite suffering more than 1,200 casualties. The site became a hotspot for tunnelling operations involving both sides.

The new month did not bring a let-up in the wet and freezing conditions with snow falling throughout the morning on March 4. Yet still the officers sent out patrols, and the artillery fire continued intermittently. On March 7, so much snow fell that a shoot arranged on enemy trenches by field guns was cancelled due to poor visibility. It was a quiet period, allowing B company to be relieved leaving D company in the line. Later the whole battalion was relieved and moved into the Brigade reserve, allowing the soldiers to rest by day and carry out work at night.

The next spell in the trenches was quieter still. During the four nights after the battalion relieved and despite enemy artillery being active for the duration, two men were killed and just three wounded. Yet the front line was not the only danger to the soldiers' lives. On March 17, the battalion proceeded to Rest Camp M in Poperinghe, Belgium. As they marched the four miles to begin a period of rest that was to last a month, two men were killed and three men were wounded. How the soldiers were afflicted is not recorded.

On March 18, the battalion began its rest, although the officers and men were not allowed to be idle. The first day consisted of a general re-fit and a much-needed clean-up, including visits to the bath house and uniform washing. By the second day, training commenced and a couple of days later, visits and inspections began by senior Army figures. On March 21, Second Army Commander Sir Herbert Plumer visited the camp. He was later to achieve a number of victories against the Germans including the Battle of Messines in 1917, when 19 near simultaneous mine explosions heralded a sizeable advance, relative to the small gains of previous years.[74] The following day Corps Commander Lord Cavan, then the Brigade Commander made inspecting visits. It was transmitted to the battalion that both officers 'expressed themselves pleased with the turn out of the battalion'.

On March 24 as training continued, Private J Brooman was awarded the Distinguished Conduct Medal and a second-lieutenant, H. B. Davies, joined to add to the officers' strength. On the evening of March 26, the battalion entrained at Poperinghe siding, and headed further away from the guns. Its strength was recorded as 22 officers, 718 other ranks and 64 horses. The infantrymen arrived at Calais, and then marched to another rest camp Beau Marais just 30 miles from England. For many of the men, including Harry, this was to be the closest they would ever again get to the country of their birth.

The rest of the month was spent in camp, the peaceful monotony broken only by the addition of another second-lieutenant and the news in the London Gazette that the commanding officer, Major G.G. Laing, had been promoted to lieutenant-colonel. On April 5, the battalion began its journey back to the front line, marching over two days to join the brigade at Wormhoudt. On arrival it was again inspected by Lord Cavan, and billeted in the area.

After another week's training, the Yorkshiremen returned to Camp M where they stayed for a night before proceeding to Canal Bank, near Ypres, where they were held in the brigade reserve. Companies A to D were split between the north and south banks of the canal, where they stayed in dugouts. Over the next four days, three men were wounded and one was killed.

On the evening of April 23, the companies moved forward and relieved the 14th Durham Light Infantry. The relief was completed by 11pm, but not before a poignant loss. Second-lieutenant H.B. Davies, who joined the battalion just a month before and was unlikely to have seen service elsewhere, was killed. He is buried at Essex Farm Cemetery north of Ypres, Belgium, alongside 1,200 other servicemen. The cemetery adjoined a field dressing station and it was in a field ambulance looking at the war graves a year earlier that Canadian Army Medical Corps Lieutenant-Colonel John McCrae wrote the poem 'In Flanders Fields':


*In Flanders fields the poppies grow*

*Between the crosses, row on row,*

*That mark our place; and in the sky*

*The larks, still bravely singing, fly*

*Scarce heard amid the guns below.*


*We are the Dead. Short days ago*

*We lived, felt dawn, saw sunset glow,*

*Loved and were loved, and now we lie*

*In Flanders fields.*


*Take up our quarrel with the foe:*

*To you from failing hands we throw*

*The torch; be yours to hold it high.*

*If ye break faith with us who die*

*We shall not sleep, though poppies grow*

*In Flanders fields*[75]

In its first spell back in the trenches after a month away from the line, five were wounded and five killed, including Captain F.W. Smith.

During April, Harry reported sick with nerves and was treated at a dressing station for two weeks before returning to font-line duty. His problems were worsening, yet the fact he was not sent far behind the lines suggest medical officers did not deem him sick enough to be evacuated. For its spell away from the line, the first battalion was stationed in dugouts and huts in the grounds of Elverdinghe Chateau and Pelissier Farm. Held in reserve, parties of four officers and about 150 men would venture out to work each night, sustaining two casualties over four days. One of those wounded was recorded as 'self-inflicted', a court martial offence although the man's fate is not recorded.

The next spell in the trenches, beginning with the relief of the Durhams on May 2, was an altogether more violent affair, with four men killed and 17 wounded during repeated bombardments. Things became particularly bad on May 4, when C Company was hit throughout the day with heavy trench mortars. The battalion diarist records that the trenches they held 'ceased to exist' and other companies were required to relieve the beleaguered soldiers.

A couple of quieter days followed before relief into the reserve area around Canal Bank. However, the movement to the rear once again did not mean a respite from the enemy. A second-lieutenant, corporal and private captured a German during an incursion into the 14th Durham Light Infantry's trenches. A number of men were also wounded as working parties toiled through the nights to repair trenches and move supplies.

The next period in the line, swapping in for the Fourteenth Battalion of the Durham regiment, was characterised by officers leaving or joining the battalion, with a handful of men falling casualty to the enemy. While a captain moved to the 18th Infantry Brigade staff, another joined, as well as two second-lieutenants.

Later, while in reserve again on May 22, two lieutenants and four second-lieutenants also joined the battalion's strength, significantly boosting the number of officers. Co-incidence or not, it meant the 750 or so soldiers of the West Yorkshires were ready for an operation that was just around the corner.

After another four-day spell in the trenches and same amount of time in reserve, the battalion was called upon to take part in a single unit operation on the night of June 3. Days earlier, senior officers had received orders to take and hold entrenchments known as the Old British Trench. Previously exited by another division, it now lay in the hands of the enemy, but was lightly defended.

The commanding officer decided to use C company made up to 200-strong with men from D company. Other members of the battalion helped before the attack, filling sandbags and some were readied to carry supplies on the night itself. A company was to be held in reserve. In the nights leading up to June 3, a reconnaissance patrol of NCOs was sent out, and on the following night officers were sent out in groups, with platoon commanders sent to examine the sector he was to seize. The target trench was up to 450 yards away, and on the night of June 3, the battalion diarist recorded: '[the] orders were carried out to the letter, except that it was impossible to wire in front of point 98 in the German line, 80 yards away owing to the deadly fire of machine guns and rifles at that close range.' The soldiers had in fact discovered the parapet in front of point 98 had been smashed by British shells, which had also obliterated the German line.

Although the division was informed that the objective had been achieved by midnight, the battalion was harassed by accurate and deadly machine gun fire, leading to the loss of platoon Second Lieutenant C.T.K. Newton who was killed and a bombing sergeant severely wounded. This incapacitating of senior soldiers led to 'confusion' that was only ended by another officer coming across to reorganise the men. Losses during the operation were heavy, with one officer and five sergeants killed, as well as five other ranks.

Two sergeants and 24 other ranks were wounded - a total casualty rate of about 17 per cent which is shockingly high. Noting in particular the toll on the sergeants, the diarist describing their loss and injuries as something the battalion 'could ill-afford'. Continuing with as much emotion as such official records permitted, he wrote: 'At the beginning of the war all these sergeants were privates and had worked their way up by hard work and merit.'

Just 24 minutes after the position was confirmed, a telegram was received from the divisional commander congratulating the battalion, and expressing sorrow for the loss of Newton. At 11am on June 4, a congratulatory telegram from the brigadier, who asked for 'best thanks and congratulations be conveyed to all concerned, particularly to the wiring parties whose gallant efforts did so much to make the captured positions secure'. For the next few days, one company remained in the line at various times, with two men killed and several wounded. The plaudits for the battalion's operation continued, this time from XIX Corps commander, who said in a letter that the attack was well organised, well carried out and a credit to the Yorkshiremen. He also noted that wet weather hindered work on improving the defences on the newly held trench.

From the commander of the Second Army, a memorandum stated that the operation was 'well planned and carried out'. Relief of the companies holding the trench continued on June 10 and another congratulatory note was received, this time from Major-General C. Ross of XI Division. On June 13, conditions were again wet, particularly at night meaning improvement of fortifications was again hindered, leaving the trench vulnerable. One man was killed, another wounded. The bad weather continued into the following day, and that night the battalion was finally relieved of all its front line duties, with the remaining company joining the rest in reserve.

On June 15, the battalion began its march to two different training camps, stopping at various points to overnight. While marching, a letter was received confirming the recent attack had led to the Military Cross being awarded to three officers, a Distinguished Conduct Medal to a corporal and a Military Medal to three men.

The next few days was spent in billets at Bollezeele, firstly digging trenches and then on June 23 undergoing attack practice on the training ground nearby. A telegram was sent to the Prince of Wales wishing him happy birthday, from the Prince of Wales' Own First Battalion West Yorkshire Regiment. In return, they received 'sincere thanks' from 'Edward'.

On June 25, a number of soldiers from the battalion were mentioned in despatches, including Company Quarter Master Booth, who was to become an important witness in the court martial conviction of Harry. The rest of the month was spent in billets, training.

Throughout 1916, a massive offensive had been planned involving both British and French troops. According to Sir Douglas Haig, the objectives were:

(1) To relieve pressure on Verdun (where the Germans continued to attack)
(2) To assist our Allies in the other theatres of war by stopping any further transfer of German troops from the Western Front
(3) To wear down the strength of the forces opposed to us[76]

On July 1st, less than 100 miles south, following a week in which 1.6m shells were fired, British forces attacked en masse on a 15-mile-long front. The slaughter that ensued on the first day of the Battle of the Somme was prodigious, with almost 60,000 British casualties, a third of them dead. News of the slaughter took days to filter back to Britain, and thanks to heavy censorship of the press the horrors of the battle were not truly expressed, but the casualty lists gave no lie the situation.

Later, those who were there would write in graphic terms of how they and their fellow soldiers suffered in that infamous attack. In One Young Man, the diary of Reginald Davis, which was published the following year, the author recounts the horrific moment he was blinded by a German shell. He said: 'We had just connected up with our party on the left when I felt a pressure of tons upon my head. My right eye was sightless, with the other I saw my hand with one finger severed, covered in blood. A great desire came over me to sink to the ground, into peaceful oblivion, but the peril of such weakness came to my mind, and with an effort I pulled myself together. I tore my helmet from my head, for the concussion had rammed it tight down. The man in front bandaged my head and eye. Blood was pouring into my mouth, down my tunic.'[77]

The editor of the diary, Sir Ernest Hodder Williams, reveals the true extent of the wounds, a 'Blighty' in common soldier parlance. He said: 'The piece of shell which entered his head just above the right eye opened up the frontal sinuses, exposing the brain. "It is wonderful," wrote the doctor who attended him, "how these fellows who have been fighting for us exhibit such a marvellous fortitude." He had lost the end of his fourth finger and another has since been entirely amputated.'[78]

Harry and his fellow soldiers of the first battalion were a long way from the massed attack on the Somme, but his former comrades in the second battalion were heavily involved. Forming part of the 8th Division, the battalion was held in support of the main infantry attack at Ovillers. But after the first two waves were mowed down by artillery and small arms fire after the initial order to attack, the Yorkshiremen were sent in to follow up.

The attack that ensued was carried out from a starting point behind the British front line and 200 officers and men were killed or injured before they even managed to reach No Man's Land. Few reached the German trenches and no ground was taken, for the horrendous loss of 500 soldiers out of a battalion strength of less than 1,000 officers and men.[79] The first day saw 100,000 British troops enter No Man's Land, of whom 20,000 were killed outright. Another 40,000 returned wounded for no real gain.[80]

Oblivious to the killing fields that they were later to join, the first battalion began its long march back towards the front. Arriving at Poperinghe on July 2, the battalion embarked upon more training and was inspected by Second Army Commander Lord Cavan, who later praised their appearance, physique and arm-drill. During this period, the battalion's strength was increased by the addition of five officers including a major. One of the new officers was a sergeant Burke who received a field commission. Three of the battalion's officers also learned that they had been awarded the Military Cross, after an announcement in the London Gazette on June 24. The officers were Captain B .Corp, Lieutenant G.N. Stockdale and Second Lieutenant H.A. Hay.

On July 15, the West Yorkshires left the camp and moved by train to Ypres where they relieved the Eleventh Battalion, Essex Regiment in a supporting role. Companies were sent to various areas called Prison, Dry Switch, Magazine, Edward Frier Street and Rue Elverdinghe. The relief was completed by 11.30pm and the next three days were spent in working and carrying parties. This was a period of minimal enemy activity, due to the German efforts in repelling the attack on the Somme.[81]

On July 19, the battalion again relieved the Essex regiment soldiers, this time in the line, in the sector between Duke Street and Fenchurch Street. The following day, D Company, holding the battalion's right side, was heavily shelled by two guns from the direction of Pilkem. One man was killed and three others were injured.

The activity dropped off for the next three days, with just one casualty in the rest of the battalion's time at the front. Worryingly, Harry again reported sick with nerves on July 22 and was detained by medical corps soldiers for the day, but this time he was returned as fit for duty the next day. On July 23 the battalion was relieved by Ninth Battalion, Suffolk Regiment and went by railway to a reserve area known as Camp B.

The next five days were spent near Vlamertinghe in the divisional reserve, cleaning, refitting and training. On July 29 a lieutenant, J.C. Davies, joined the battalion, and two days later, it left the camp and took a light railway journey to billets in Wormhoudt. Training continued there before the West Yorkshires left the billets at 4.30pm on August 2 and marched to Esquelbec where the strength of 28 officers and 868 men travelled to Doullens via Hazebrouck, arriving after midnight. The final route march took them to Orville, and fresh billets, where the battalion stayed for two days and nights before marching in brigade formation for seven miles to Acheux, where it remained in camp for two nights.

On August 6, camp was broken and the battalion marched to Mailly-Maillet, where dinners were served. That afternoon, at 3pm, the West Yorkshire filed into trenches held by the Third Battalion of the Worcestershire Regiment, one platoon at a time. The battalion had joined the Battle of the Somme, infamous for the unprecedented British losses and intensity of the shelling operation. According to the historian Stevenson, 'the fighting here was even more concentrated than at Verdun, the British and Germans firing a total of 30 million shells at each other. It rivalled Verdun in the number of deaths per square yard'.[82]

Two companies, B and C, took up positions on the front line while two more were held in support, completing the move by 7pm. The trench occupied was known as Gordon Trench and the section was between Long Acre and Louvercy Street. The following day, the British activity was noted as being very active, 'cutting wire and shelling'. At the same time, the battalion suffered 12 casualties – two dead and 10 wounded – including Second-Lieutenant J.W. Mather. The wire cutting activities continued the next day but enemy activity dropped off, leaving the battalion without casualties.

On August 9 the West Yorkshires were removed from the line, relieved by First Battalion, The Buffs, of the 16th Infantry Brigade, with all members of the battalion away from the line and in billets in Englebelmer by 4.30pm. That evening seven officers and 270 other ranks were sent on a working party. The following day was spent in the brigade reserve, still at Englebelmer. The billets sustained shelling between 9 and 10pm. During the course of the day, eight officers and 400 men were sent on a working party, and one man was killed and another wounded.

The week that followed was also spent in reserve, with the battalion continuing to provide working parties on an almost daily basis. On August 13, more than 400 officers and men were sent to carry out work, while Second-Lieutenant C.S. Gell joined the battalion. The following day, the same number of soldiers were sent for digging duties, during which one man was killed. The battalion diarist also recorded the temporary promotion of Second-Lieutenant W. Paul, who was to become the adjutant, and hold the rank of lieutenant while doing so, in the place of Captain F.A.W. Armitage.

The next four days were spent in the brigade reserve as before, with hundreds of men sent on digging and carrying duties. This work proved more hazardous than the previous week, with four killed, nine wounded and one man missing, 'believed to have been blown up'. Those killed and eight of the wounded were all victims on the same day, 15 August.

On August 19, it was confirmed that Second-Lieutenant J.F. Wallace was to be made temporary adjutant of No 3 Infantry Base Depot in Rouen, in the place of a captain. In the afternoon the battalion was sent to the front to relieve the Fourteenth Battalion, Durham Light Infantry. The movement was completed by 5pm and the West Yorkshires held the left sub-section of the brigade's trenches.

The next day the battalion came under fire from the German artillery. In particular, the soldiers were harassed by minenwerfer, German trench mortars capable of remarkable accuracy at a variety of ranges. One man was killed during the peak firing times, 11.15pm to 11.45pm and for another 30-minute spell shortly after midnight. The next two nights followed a similar pattern, with four men wounded over the two days. The trenches were also the target of occasional shelling during the day on August 22.

The next day the sector was hit by a constant bombardment, with the Germans zeroing in on the communication trenches that ran from the reserve lines to the front. Three men were wounded. August 24 was a quiet day, with just one casualty, but the day after saw the heavy shelling of A company during the morning, leaving one wounded.

On August 26, the battalion was relieved by the First Battalion, Cambridgeshire Regiment. All of the soldiers were out of the line by 4.30pm, and they proceeded to a camp at Betrancourt. One man was wounded during the day. The next day the West Yorkshires joined the brigade in marching eight miles to Amplier, arriving at 1pm where it entered a camp. One man was killed during the movement. The next day the brigade continued its march, arriving at Hem, six miles away, at about 11.30am, where soldiers were stationed in billets. Its final destination on the march was reached the next morning, when the brigade travelled a further 13 miles, arriving before 2pm in Vignacourt. The last two days of the month were spent there, in training and a 'general clean up'.

This period of rest, recuperation and training continued into September, with five full days in the same billets. On September 6, the West Yorkshires headed to Rainneville alongside the rest of the brigade to take over billets, having marched 10 miles before 2pm. Again the long marches among other units of the brigade continued, with the battalion covering 14 miles to Vaux-on-Somme, arriving at 2pm and entering billets. The next three whole days were spent in training while staying in the same accommodation.

On September 11, the battalion proceeded with the brigade to an area known as Sandpits, arriving at a camp at 5.30pm, before taking a three-mile route march to a camp at Citadel, where it remained for another day. On September 14 the West Yorkshiremen marched another three miles, before taking to bivouacs. From there, at 1am the next morning, the battalion moved up towards the fighting. The soldiers took up positions in Chimpanzee trench, in the brigade reserve. Nine men were wounded, a small taste of the carnage they were days away from facing.

The following day was spent in the brigade reserve, in the area near Guillemont. Six men were killed and four more were wounded amid a general British offensive across the sector, involving the use of the latest weapon – tanks.[83] On September 16, the battalion moved into the front line trenches, relieving the Second Battalion, Durham Light Infantry at the north end of an area named the Quadrilateral by the British Army.

The relief took place into the early hours of September 17, and was completed by 3am. Later that day, two Royal Army Medical Corp captains joined the unit, D.B. Chiles-Evans and W. Williams. If the men were unaware before that an attack was imminent, the presence of these officers would have revealed what was ahead. During the day one man was killed another was wounded.

On September 18, the battalion joined others of the VI Division in attacking the opposing trenches in the Quadrilateral, 'a fortified point that had held up the whole British attack for months'.[84] The attack was part of a larger action known as the battle of Flers-Courcelette, the third phase of the Battle of the Somme.

At 5.50am, whistles sounded along the line as the soldiers poured up and over the front trenches, through previously cut barbed wire and between breastworks. Within six minutes, D company, commanded by G.N. Stockdale, M.C., began their bombing attack of the German line. They were armed with Mills bombs, and would have attempted to lob them into the German trenches and dugouts after activating the time-delayed fuse. Meanwhile, B and C companies led by Captains B. Corp and J.H.E. Trafford-Rawson attacked front-on, marching straight into the teeth of German guns.

The companies were met with 'very heavy' machine gun and rifle fire and were forced to retreat back to the trenches where the attack started from. Ten minutes into the attack, two platoons from A company advanced across the German trenches, reaching a quarry, 250 yards in front of the Quadrilateral. Within 15 minutes, at 6.15am, the platoons were digging new positions at the quarry. D company grenadiers were succeeding in their daring raid, and by 6.10am had captured an enemy strong-point. While bombing along a trench, rather than into it, they met with soldiers from the Fourteenth Battalion, Durham Light Infantry, whom the West Yorkshires had relieved in front line trenches the previous month. At the same time that the two battalions linked up in the enemy trenches, reorganised B and C companies attacked again and this time took the trenches opposite them, and advanced 'on, over the crest'. The soldiers met up with their comrades – the Durhams on the left and A company on the right. They then proceeded to dig in at 6.15am. A company held its position with a Lewis Gun and two platoons manning a captured strong point. It had also managed to send out patrols, which made contact with soldiers from the 20th Division. The company's left flank was protected by two machine guns.

Meanwhile, D company was also consolidating its position, making four new strong points. All of the companies were then subjected to intense bombardments by the Germans, desperate to force them out of the captured positions. The attack was successful and could be measured both in ground and trenches captured as well as material and men. The West Yorkshires counted one trench mortar, one machine gun and 100 prisoners, both wounded and unharmed, taken at the end of the attack. But the cost was shockingly high, with more than 100 casualties across the battalion, an attrition rate of more than 10 per cent. Among the 13 dead were three officers, Captain B. Corp who led B company in the attack and Second-Lieutenants M. Burke and C.S. Gell, the latter of whom had joined the battalion just one month earlier. Almost 100 soldiers were wounded, including four officers. This was just one of scores of small-scale actions that made up the battle, leaving thousands dead and injured but without a major breakthrough.

The companies held their positions until 4am when relief by the 5th Division was completed and they made their way to bivouacs. As the soldiers rested, command of the First West Yorkshire battalion was assumed by Major H.M. Dillon, of the Second Battalion, Oxfordshire and Buckinghamshire Light Infantry. He took over from Lieutenant-Colonel G.G. Laing DSO. The battalion diary records that he was taken to hospital but does not note what for. He was not listed among the wounded during the attack.

Later on September 19, the exhausted soldiers made their way to billets in Meaulte, eight miles away, where they remained overnight and the following day. The attack was considered a success, but Private Farr had not taken part in the operation. His final nervous collapse took place on September 17.

Harry had fallen out sick on September 16, yet when he made his way to a dressing station the following day he was not seen because he was not wounded. On September 17 he was ordered to the front, in the company of a rations party, but was found at 11pm that night at the same place behind the lines, having disobeyed the order. When he was subsequently sent to the front under escort, he struggled with his guards and was released after refusing to see a medical officer further forward.

Harry ran back towards the transport lines in the rear and was held under guard before being placed under arrest on September 18 and later charged with cowardice. The timing of his collapse – ahead of the impending attack, may have helped along the decision to charge him.

The Battle of the Somme resulted in the greatest loss of life in military history at that time, for negligible gains.[85] Across the whole offensive during that awful summer and autumn, between July 1 and November 19, the British Army suffered 420,000 casualties, the French 195,000 and the German losses stood at between 500,000 and 650,000.[86]

## Chapter Four

On October 2, 1916, Private Harry Farr stood trial by Field General Court Martial, which was convened at Vill-Sur-Ancre, France. Since his nervous collapse and arrest, his battalion had again been in action following their part in the success in the capture of the Quadrilateral. This time they had helped attack and take the village of Leboeufs on September 25, part of the wider Battle of Morval[87]. It was against this backdrop of missing two significant actions that Harry was tried.

A Field General Court Martial was a wartime disciplinary tribunal with the power to try all military offences and hand down the ultimate sanction, the death penalty. It required at least three officers to sit in judgment including a president. If passing the death sentence, all members had to agree.[88] Those sitting in judgment were the president, Lieutenant-Colonel Frederick Swing of Eleventh Battalion, Essex Regiment, Captain James Jones of Second Battalion, Durham Light Infantry and Lieutenant C. A. V. Newsome of Fourteenth Battalion, Durham Light Infantry.[89] Lieutenant-Colonel Swing, DSO, had seen service in the Boer War and did a stint as an embarkation officer at the start of the war before serving as a Brigade Major and a Staff Officer in Europe. Captain Jones, MC, had served in the ranks for almost 20 years before he was promoted to Second-Lieutenant in October 1914, he rose higher the following year with a further two promotions. Captain Newsome MC appeared to have joined the Army at the outbreak of the war. He became a Major but was badly wounded and it is believed he died in 1925.[90]

Harry was charged with an offence contrary to section 4. (7) of the Army Act 1881. The exact charge was 'misbehaving before the enemy in such a manner as to show cowardice', to which he pleaded not guilty. The format of the hearing was different to British criminal law, being inquisitorial rather than adversarial. In courts martial, prosecution cases were put forward first, with witnesses called to give evidence on oath. The accused or his chosen defending officer was then allowed to cross-examine the witnesses and call their own as they made their case. However, Harry appeared without a 'prisoner's friend'. Finally, both sides were given the opportunity to sum up their cases, with the accused's side given the last word.[91]

The evidence put before the panel appeared damning from the start. A note, written in the field by the officer commanding A Company, Captain A. Wiltow, stated that the soldier had come out with the second battalion, and was sent back to the base 'with shell-shock, 9.5.15'. He wrote that Harry rejoined the regiment, this time with the first battalion, on October 20 1915, and had remained with it.

Assessing his overall situation, Captain Wiltow said: 'I cannot say what has destroyed this man's nerves but he has proved himself on many occasions incapable of keeping his head in action and likely to cause a panic.' However, the officer made a point of differentiating between these problems and the unfortunate soldier's nature, saying: 'Apart from his behaviour his conduct and character are very good.'

The next piece of evidence was signed by W. William, the battalion's medical officer. He wrote: 'I hereby certify that I examined no. 8871 Pt H Farr, 1st Btn Yorks. On October 2nd1916 and that in my opinion both the general physical and mental condition were satisfactory.' Interestingly, the word good appears before the word satisfactory, but is struck out by the same hand, indicating some doubts in the officer's mind.

The trial began formally with a prosecution witness, Regimental Sergeant Major H. Laking, who said: 'On 17th Sept 1916 about 9am the accused reported himself to me at A Line transport – he states he was sick and had fallen out from his company the night previous on the march up to the trenches. He states he could not find his company commander for permission to fall out. I order him to report to the dressing station.

'When he returns he states they would not see him as he was not wounded. I then order him to proceed to the battalion with the ration party which was going in the evening. The ration party paraded about 8pm – the accused was present and marched off with it. On arrival at the ration dump Co QMS Booth reported to me [that the accused was missing].

'On returning to the first line for about 11pm I saw the accused standing near a brazier. I asked him why he was there. He replies "I cannot stand it." I ask him what he meant. He again replies "I cannot stand it". I told him he would have to go to the trenches that night. He replies "I cannot go". I order Co QMS Booth to take him up to the trenches under escort. After going 500 yards the accused commences to scream and struggle with his escort. I again warned him that he would have to go to the trenches or be tried for cowardice.

'He replied "I am not fit to go to the trenches". I then said I would take him to see a medical officer – he refused to go saying "I will not go any further that way." I ordered the escort to take him on - the accused again started struggling and screaming. I ordered the escort to leave him alone when he jumped up and ran back to the 1st Line Transport. I placed him in charge of a guard at the 1st Line Transport.'

The second witness to be called was Company Quarter Master Sergeant J.W. Booth of the First Battalion, West Yorkshire Regiment. He appears to have survived the war.

He said: 'On 17th September 1916 about 3pm I ordered the accused to parade with carrying party at 6pm to go up and join his company in the trenches. The accused paraded and marched off with the ration party. On arrival at the ration dump the accused was absent having fallen out on the way up without permission. About 9pm I saw the accused near the 1st Line Transport. The Regimental Sergeant Major ordered me to take the accused with escort to the trenches. 'About 500 yards from the 1st Line Transport the accused became violent, threatened the escort and eventually broke away, returning to the 1st Line Transport. The Regimental Sergeant Major ordered me to place the accused in charge of a guard.'

The third witness was Private D. Farrar, who also appears to have survived the war. He said: 'On 17th September 1916 about 11.30pm I was ordered by Company Quarter Master Sergeant Booth to form part of an escort to take the accused up to his company in the trenches. After going about 500 yards the accused started struggling and saying he wanted to see a doctor. The sergeant major said he would see one when he got a bit further up. The accused refused to go any further. I tried to pull him along. The sergeant major told me to let him go and the accused went back to the 1st Line Transport.'

The next witness was Lance-Corporal W Form, of the First West Yorkshire Regiment. He said he was also detailed by the Company Quarter Master to escort Harry to the trenches, and to take charge. He said: 'After going 500 yards the accused became violent and started shouting and eventually broke away from the escort. We followed him and found him at the First Line Transport. The Regimental Sergeant Major then ordered me to be in charge of a guard over the accused.'

In his defence, Private Farr said: 'On 16th September 1916 when going up to the trenches with my company I fell out sick. I could not find the company officer to obtain permission, the sergeant I asked has now been wounded. I went back to the First Line Transport arriving there about 2am on 17th September 1916. I would have reported at once to the Regimental Sergeant Major only I was told he was asleep. I reported about 9am on 17th September.

'The Sergeant Major told me to go to the advanced dressing station, they however would not see me there as I was not wounded. The Sergeant Major told me to go up with the ration party at night. I started with this party and had to fall out sick. I could not get permission as I was in the rear and the Sergeant Major was in the front, but left word with a private soldier. I returned to 1st Line Transport hoping to report sick to some medical officer there.

'On the Sergeant Major's return I reported to him and said I was sick and could not stand it. He then said "you are a fucking coward and you will go to the trenches. I give fuck all for my life and I give fuck all for yours and I'll get you fucking well shot." The Sergeant Major, Company Quarter Master Booth and Private Farrar then took me towards the trenches. We went about a mile when we met a carrying party returning under Lance-Corporal Form.

'The Sergeant Major asked Lance-Corporal Form where I was and he replied "run away, same as last night". I said to the Sergeant Major "you have got this all made up for me." The Sergeant Major then told Lance-Corporal Form to fall out two men and take me to the trenches. They commenced to shove me. I told them not to as I was sick enough as it was.

'The Sergeant Major then grabbed my rifle and said "I'll blow your fucking brains out if you don't go." I then called out for an officer but there was none there. I was then tripped up and commenced to struggle. After this I do not know what happened until I found myself back in the First Line Transport under a guard. If the escort had not started to shove me about I would have gone up to the trenches. It was on account of their doing this that I commenced to struggle.'

After the statement, Harry was cross-examined by the court's prosecutor, who asked if he had had the opportunity of reporting sick since September 16. Harry replied: 'Yes, after I was put under arrest on 18th September.' A member of the court martial panel then asked why he had not reported sick since his arrest, to which he replied, fatefully: 'Because being away from the shell fire I felt better.'

In previous courts martial for desertion, nervous conditions due to battle conditions were not accepted as a defence and in January 1916 a 19-year-old soldier was executed despite pleading that his mind had been affected by heavy shelling.[92] The first witness called by the defence other than Harry was Sergeant J. Andrews, of the same battalion. He said: 'The accused reported sick with nerves about April 1916 – the medical officer retained him for about a fortnight in the dressing station. He reported again for the same cause on 22.7.16 and was retained for all the day, but was discharged for duty the following day.'

The medical officer Captain Evans of the Royal Army Medical Corps who saw him had since been wounded. Indeed medical officers were renowned for taking a no-nonsense approach when confronted with cases of sickness in or near the front line. Some would even go as far as to ensure they gave evidence against men accused of cowardice and desertion because they felt that those who claimed to be sick in the face of dangerous conditions or enemy action deserved to be shot.[93]

Evidence as to the character of Private Farr was presented to the court. The battalion's adjutant, Lieutenant W. Paul, stated that he knew Harry for six weeks. He said: 'On working parties he has three times asked for leave to fall out and return to camp as he could not stand the noise of the artillery. He was trembling and did not appear to be in a fit state.'

Harry's conduct sheet was presented to the court, with the only misdemeanour appearing to be an 'overstayed pass from 12 midnight until 7.30pm on November 3rd, 1914'. It referred to the day before he was due to ship out to France, when Harry had returned to camp the best part of a day late. Though this was inexcusable in the eyes of the military authorities it was more likely to be a result of chaotic transportation across the south of England with the country thrown into war just a few months earlier.

The first modern assessment of the court martial documents belonging to Harry and the 306 other men shot at dawn for offences such as cowardice was by Judge Anthony Babington, granted special access to them in 1985 when they were still held in the National Archives as 'restricted documents'. Addressing other cases in which soldiers were tried for capital offences, Judge Babington said: 'It seems wrong that when the lives of the prisoners were at stake that the members of the courts which were trying them should not have received the clearest elucidation of the law from a legally qualified adviser.'[94]

So the very process of trial was flawed, according to Judge Babington and addressing Harry's case he described it as 'particularly disquieting'. He noted Harry's length of service, and how he returned to base suffering from shell-shock in May 1915. He said: 'Obviously he had not fully recovered.' He went on: 'The Yorkshire soldier was condemned to death and shot without being examined by a doctor. Perhaps this was in accordance with what had become general policy. According to Robert Graves, during the summer of 1916, an Army order, secret and confidential, was circulated to all officers of the rank of captain and above informing them that cases of cowardice were always to be punished by death and that no medical excuses were to be accepted.'[95]

Julian Putkowski, who with Julian Sykes wrote Shot At Dawn, the first book to name the soldiers executed for military offences, was also able to list a number of factors he believed were causes for concern when reviewing Harry's case.

They included the fact that he appeared undefended and that there was no evidence to suggest he was offered the opportunity to have a defending officer; that the court was not advised by a Judge Advocate despite one seemingly being available; that the court accepted evidence from the prosecution without question; that senior officers tasked with confirming the sentence had accepted hearsay as evidence; and that Harry was known to be suffering from shell-shock and the effects of the condition were well known to high-ranking commanders in the field.[96]

Indeed Mr Putkowski cited a letter from Sir Aylmer Hunter-Weston, Commander VIII Corps in Gallipoli and France to Lieutenant-Colonel Clive Wigram in June 1915. In it, Hunter-Weston writes: 'The ding-dong fighting and constant exposure to fire night and day has an effect on most men's nerves and more than one of the senior officers: - brigade and battalion commanders, have broken down under the strain. It is marvellous how quickly most officers and men, who have not gone over breaking point, recover after a good night's sleep and a couple of days' rest...

'When men get really physically exhausted to near the limit of human endurance, almost every man's mind and strength of will go and some become jabbering idiots, as occurred to a very gallant young officer the other day. Fortunately that young officer was able to get 14 hours continuous sleep after being taken away from the front line and this saved him and made him quite fit again.'[97]

Private Harry Farr was sentenced to death. The wording on the charge sheet was stark. Under a column entitled Finding and if Convicted, Sentence; two words were handwritten in pencil. GUILTY. DEATH. There was no right to an appeal, but there was the prospect of the death penalty being commuted by the commander-in-chief who had to confirm it after reading the comments of senior officers who also looked at the file.[98]

| Offence charged | Plea | Finding, and if Convicted, Sentence (b) | How dealt with by Confirming Officer |
|---|---|---|---|
| Section 4.(7) AA.<br><br>Misbehaving before the enemy in such a manner as to show cowardice. | Not Guilty | GUILTY.<br><br>DEATH. | *[signatures]* Reserved<br><br>Bn. Comy/18 B.<br><br>Confirmed<br>*[signature]*<br>14 Oct: 16 |

D E A T H    C E R T I F I C A T E .

- - - - - - - - - - - - - - - - - - - - - - - - - - - - - - - - - -

     I certify that No: 8871, Private HARRY FARR of

1st Bn: West Yorkshire Regiment was executed by shooting

at 6 a.m. on 18th October, 1916, at CARNOY.

     Death was instantaneous.

*R Anderson Capt R.A.M.C.*
*M.O/c 6 D.A.C*

These officers – brigade, division, army and corps commanders - were in turn asked for their opinion on the case, and all supported the death penalty. The officer commanding 14th Corps, Lieutenant-General the Earl of Cavan, was emphatic when supporting the ultimate sanction. He wrote: 'The charge of cowardice seems to be clearly proven and the sergeant major's opinion of the man is definitely bad to say the least of it. The G.O.C. XI Division informs me the men know the man is no good. I therefore recommend that the sentence be carried out.' The papers finally landed on the desk of Field Marshal Haig, who signed his name on them on October 14, 12 days after the trial. By this stage the First Battalion, West Yorkshire Regiment had taken part in two further offensives in the Somme region following the Battle of Flers-Courcelette, which Harry had missed due to his arrest. They had fought at the Battle of Morval and were currently engaged in the Battle of Le Transloy, which was the last big effort of the Battle of the Somme. On October 12, the battalion had suffered heavily during an action known as the Attack on Mild and Cloudy Trenches in front of the village of Gueudecourt.[99] Against intense opposition featuring concentrated machine gun and rifle fire and suffering from shelling by both the Germans and their own artillery due to an error, the attack failed. Two officers were wounded, 24 other ranks were killed, 71 were wounded and 10 posted as missing.[100] It was against this backdrop the Earl Haig was asked to take the decision whether to confirm the death penalty. According to Corrigan, 'The Commander-in-Chief had to take into account not only the views of the accused's superiors but also the prevailing conditions.'[101]

In his meticulous war diaries, no mention was made of his decision to endorse the sentence of the court. Early in the war he established a hard line against deserters, having witnessed soldiers leaving the battlefield without authority as early as November 1914, before Harry's battalion had even arrived in France. He wrote: 'The Lincolns, Northumberlands and Bedfords left the trenches on account of a little shellfire... I order all men to be tried by court martial who have funked in this way.'[102]

On March 3 the following year, Haig recorded that he had recommended that three men of the Loyal North Lancashire regiment be shot for desertion, after one was found as far away as Paris. However, the executions were never carried out.[103] On the day that Harry died, the then-commander of British forces wrote: 'Mr John Masefield came to lunch. He is a poet but I am told he has written the best account of our landing in Gallipoli. Now he wishes to write about the deeds of our men in the Battle of the Somme. To this I readily agreed.' He said that he would help the writer gain access to those with first-hand information about the battle, presumably without such detail as those shot to death by their comrades.[104]

In Harry's bundle of court martial papers, two other important documents reside. One is a certificate confirming his fitness to stand trial. The other is his death certificate. After the court martial, he remained in custody until he was tied to a post and shot at dawn, by a firing squad.

Harry had spent four years in the service of his country,
two years before the war, and two during it. During those
years between November 1914 when he arrived in France
and his death in October 1916, the private soldier took part
in a number of actions with his infantry battalion, most
notably the Battle of Neuve Chappelle.

It was one of the most intense and attritional chapters of
the entire conflict on the Western Front, one of the first
examples of the wholesale slaughter of British troops, for
which the First World War has become renowned. Within
months he was in hospital, his nerves shattered with a
diagnosis of shell-shock.

Yet he returned to the Front in October 1915 and fought on
for another 11 months, with two more spells of sickness
because of his shell-shock. According to Chris Walsh in
Cowardice – A Brief History: 'As World War One
"dragged on", Captain Charles Wilson of the Royal Army
Medical Corps observed "fear was no longer an occasional
and exotic visitor but a settler in our midst."

'Its cumulative effect led Wilson (later Lord Moran, Sir Winston Churchill's personal doctor) to think that a man's ability to hold up against it – his courage – was not absolute quality of his character but something he had a certain amount of, like money in a bank account, and which could be depleted slowly or suddenly by the hardships and horrors of war.'[105]

Harry Farr had reached the limit of his endurance and could go no further. Despite his record of service, his repeated treatment for a recognised illness and claims that no shell-shocked soldier was being executed, he was tied against a post and shot to death in what would become one of the most infamous British punishments of the war.

---

In late 1916, a telegram arrived for Gertrude Farr from the War Office. Opening the envelope with trembling hands and a thumping heart, she read the bold, type-written message that realised her worst fears. Harry Farr had died in France. But not in battle, or of wounds sustained under fire. Re-reading it in disbelief, Gertrude learned that her husband had been executed by firing squad. The stark message read: 'We regret to inform you that Harry Thomas Farr of the First West Yorkshire Regiment has been shot for showing cowardice in the face of the enemy.' His shocking death came against a background of fervent militarism in Britain. Though shaken by the industrial levels of casualties sustained during the summer's failed Somme campaign in which hundreds of thousands of young British men had died, there was still a public appetite for the war.

The losses during the Battle of the Somme were unprecedented and had a subduing effect on British Home Front morale. Even in the present day, war memorials show that even the smallest hamlets failed to escape the killing of their inhabitants. Yet a defiant attitude of patriotism remained and 'in the mood of the moment little sympathy was wasted on those deemed to be "shirkers" or "funks"'.[106]

Worse, since 1914 when Admiral Charles Fitzgerald set up the Order of the White Feather – an organised effort to use women to shame men into volunteering for service using white feathers to symbolise cowardice – there was a real feeling against those seen to be shirking their responsibilities. Though Harry could not have been accused of failing his country in his service, his death, with its vague detail, would have meant people would assume he let his mates down.

Cowardice was the dirtiest of words and that is why the telegram proved so devastating to his widow, on top of the terrible news of his death. Later Gertrude would recount to her granddaughter Janet how she felt sick to her stomach, how she questioned how Harry, a former regular soldier, a volunteer who had fought since almost the beginning, could be considered a coward.

And then she resolved to never tell anyone how her husband had died, tucking the telegram into her blouse and with it, she hoped, the secret. She said: 'I didn't want nobody to know what had happened.

'Nobody knew, I wouldn't tell anybody. I don't know, I thought it was so terrible I suppose. I felt it was so awful, I felt it was on my shoulders, all that stigma. That's how I felt.'[107]

Such a powerful sense of shame has been utilised for centuries to ensure soldiers did their duty. According to Chris Walsh in Cowardice – A Brief history: 'Shame… constitutes a powerful deterrent to cowardice. It escalates social pressure so effectively that society need do little work, so deeply has the individual absorbed its moral code. The shame of cowardice can go well beyond the self to affect one's kin – living, dead, and yet to be born. A Union soldier wrote to a wife of a captain's cowardice, "what a stigma for men to transmit to their posterity, your father a coward". A 1915 British recruiting poster showed a man haunted by the prospect of his daughter asking him, "Daddy, what did YOU do in the Great War?"'[108]

In the weeks and months that followed, Gertrude, now a war widow in the eyes of friends and family, continued to do her best for her and Harry's little daughter, Gertie, now aged three. Separation Allowances, paid to all dependents of soldiers, continued to be paid for 26 weeks after a man died[109], and Gertrude's allowance was enough to pay their rent, food and buy clothes for Gertie.

Yet one week when she arrived at the Post Office to collect her handful of shillings, she was told: 'Sorry Mrs Farr, there's no money for you today.' Further investigation showed that in line with government policy, the family of a man shot for cowardice had been cut off by the state. War widows' pensions were not paid automatically and at this stage of the war, they were not paid to wives of those executed for military offences.

No effort was made to hide the fact that soldiers were shot following courts martial from their families. However, this was not deliberate transparency. According to historian Basil Liddell Hart: 'I had imagined, like most soldiers, that such executions were camouflaged in some way as accidental death. When I protested at the callousness of these bald announcements, I was told it was a means of saving the government's money on pensions.'[110]

Consideration at the highest level had also been given to the fact that relatives would eventually learn of their loved-one's fate, through fellow soldiers or even worse, rumours.

The pension issue meant within the space of a few months, Gertrude had been left with nothing and was cast out on the street by her landlord when she couldn't pay the rent. Gertrude turned to her friend Alice who took them in, but the young widow began to grow thin as she worried about her perilous situation. She decided to visit the Soldiers' and Sailors' Families Association, which was later to become the modern day charity SSAFA. Their kindly staff said they would try to find her employment, and advised her to tell her family of her plight. She said: 'My dear mother didn't know, nor his mother, not until the time when my pension was stopped. Then I had to tell them because they wanted to know why I was ill and upset, then I had to tell them.'[111]

It was news that was not received well by Harry's father who was overcome with shame. Fearing the stigma associated with Harry's death, he never spoke to Gertrude or his granddaughter again and forbade mention of Harry's name by anyone else in the family.

During this period, Gertrude was visited by her parish clergyman, from Christ Church, Kensington. The vicar told her that he had been in contact with the padre of Harry's battalion, and that he had witnessed the execution. According to the military chaplain, Harry had refused to wear a blindfold when he faced the firing squad.

This news was a crumb of comfort to Gertrude, who would never accept her husband was a coward. For the first time, the vicar revealed a few details of Harry's demise and the events leading up to it, including the padre's belief that he was suffering from shell-shock and that in light of his decision not to wear a blindfold, was in fact a very brave man.

Eventually Gertrude was offered work by the Scottish woman owner of a large house in Ewell, Surrey, and the SSFA offered to put little Gertie into a home. However, the household agreed for Gertie to stay with her mother, and Gertrude began work as a kitchen maid. The hours were long, the work hard but they were together, with their immediate future secured. Gertrude was paid seven shillings a month on top of her and her daughter's bed and board, about a quarter of what Harry was earning while fighting on the Western Front.

Against their father's insistence, Harry's brothers came to visit their sister-in-law and niece at Spring House as it was called. On one occasion, they helped themselves to peaches from its walled garden, drawing the ire of the lady of the house. Despite their visits, Gertrude felt isolated in the house and was drawn back to her native London after a year, taking up a position in a grand town house in Hampstead belonging to Lord and Lady Arkwright. Already working in the three-storey red brick house was Gertrude's sister-in-law, employed as a dressmaker. She informed Gertrude of the vacancy for a general maid, and spoke to Lady Arkwright of Gertrude's tragic circumstances, which elicited great sympathy.

Lord and Lady Arkwright had three daughters of their own and were happy for little Gertie to join them in the house. Recounting her time employed in the house more than 70 years later, Gertrude said she could not have worked for a nicer couple. She described Lady Arkwright as a very tall, gaunt woman with a firm voice but a pleasing manner. Thanks to her and her husband, Gertie was to enjoy a privileged upbringing and a far better education than if she had attended her local school.

The young Arkwright girls - Elizabeth, Anne and Bridget - were taught their lessons by a governess and young Gertie was allowed to sit in on the classes. According to Gertie, sometimes the girls were unkind and would make fun of her, especially if she was wearing one of their old dresses that had been handed down. On one occasion young Gertie was wearing a pair of shoes that had belonged to Bridget. When the young mistress saw Gertie wearing her old shoes she threw such a tantrum that she was made to take the shoes off and give them back to Bridget.

Another instance of mild ill-treatment was when one of the girls cut Gertie's fringe, making a bad job of it and leaving it crooked. Gertie also remembers how the sisters delighted in making her walk along the top of a low wall in the garden, hoping she would fall off and hurt herself. The children's nursery was a place of wonder to Gertie, filled with expensive toys such as beautiful dolls, a huge dolls' house, china tea sets and teddy bears. The centre-piece of the room was a large rocking horse, making it a magical place for young Gertie, who despite being surrounded by such wealth, never had a doll of her own. But the nursery also contained hundreds of books, from the complete works of Beatrice Potter housed in a carousel, to the latest stories by famous children's authors.

Despite her fortunate position as a fourth child in the house, Gertrude feared her daughter would cause trouble for them both if she disturbed the other members of the household staff, or the family. Little Gertie was never allowed to cry, and was told sternly by her mother: 'Don't let the cook hear you crying otherwise I will be out of a job.'

Every Sunday without fail the Arkwright family would attend the service in the church at the end of Church Row. The whole family would be chauffeur-driven the short distance to the church in the family car. Young Gertie was always included in the family group. She would follow behind the three young mistresses and sat in the family pew with them. Lord Arkwright is believed to have made his fortune through the family glass manufacturing business and there is an Arkwright Road in Hampstead named after the family.

Gertrude felt that after the past few traumatic years and the shocking and dreadful death of Harry, life was now beginning to change for the better. She was fortunate to have employers who were good to them both, and she and Gertie were well fed and had a comfortable bed to sleep in at night. They both slept in a room at the top of the house, which they had to share with the housemaid. However, for little Gertie, that room was a lonely place where she spent many hours by herself. Catching childhood ailments such as chicken pox and measles resulted her being confined to the room while her mother worked downstairs. A cotton sheet dipped in disinfectant would be draped over the bedroom door to keep any germs from being transferred around the house.

One incident keenly remembered by Gertrude decades later concerned the theft of eggs from a large storage jar in the pantry. The cook noticed that eggs seemed to be going missing and leading from the jar were wet marks on the stone tiles in the pantry. Unfortunately, the finger was pointed at Gertrude. It was thought that she was taking the eggs for her young daughter, Gertie. Gertrude was summoned to the drawing room and questioned by the master of the house regarding the disappearing eggs. She denied emphatically that she would never stoop so low as to steal from her employer.

Still the eggs went missing – so Gertrude decided to find out who the thief was and to clear her own name. She had her suspicions and believed it to be the dressmaker, her own sister-in-law. When Gertrude cleaned the woman's room she decided to have a good look around. There under the bed was an old suitcase and when Gertrude took a look inside she could not believe her eyes.

Inside the case she found cigarettes, apples, off-cuts of material and many other items and, of course, the stolen eggs. She was so furious with her sister-in-law for putting the blame on her that Gertrude kicked the case so hard she broke all the eggs, the gooey mess going all over the other stolen goods in the case. The police were called and the sister-in-law owned up to the theft and was immediately dismissed.

One evening Gertrude was asked to wait at table because it was the parlour maid's evening off. The household were short-staffed due to the fact that many of the male servants or footmen were serving as soldiers in France. Lord and Lady Arkwright had some very distinguished guests for supper that evening. The Earl and Countess of Clarendon were the special guests and Gertrude felt very privileged to be asked wait on them.

The Earl had entered the House of Lords in 1914 upon his father's death and was later made Conservative Chief Whip in the chamber.[112] When they had finished their meal the Earl asked to speak to Gertrude. She was very nervous thinking that perhaps she had done something to displease him but the Earl explained he wanted to discuss the unfortunate circumstances regarding Harry's death.

Lord Arkwright had spoken to the Earl about Gertrude's situation regarding her not receiving a pension from the Army because Harry had been executed. The Earl told Gertrude that he was very interested in her case and that he had contacts in the War Office who might be able to help her. Perhaps he could put her case to them and try to get her some financial assistance. The Earl asked Gertrude for any letters, the telegram announcing Harry's death or field cards that he could use as proof of circumstances. The outcome of his appeal was that he managed to get a child allowance for young Gertie.

The papers handed to the War Office and Ministry of Pensions were never returned and despite appeals to the government department responsible for pensions in the early 1990s, the documents including all the letters sent home by Harry were never located. Janet Booth, Gertrude's granddaughter, was later told that many of the records, including Harry's medical records, had been lost during the Second World War. During the Blitz an incendiary bomb fell on the War Office Record Store in Arnside Street, London, leading to a hugely damaging fire, which destroyed more than two million documents relating to First World War soldiers.

In 1921 Gertrude married William Batstone, an old school friend of Harry, who had also fought for his country during the war. William suffered from asthma, which had been exacerbated by him inhaling mustard gas while in the trenches in the France. Little Gertie was eight years old when Gertrude and William married and they moved back to North Kensington.

They had two children of their own – Edward and Margary. Gertie always said that William was a wonderful step-father. He was the father figure she had never had, but William was never truly well again and died during the Second World War. Gertrude was once again widowed, and Gertie left without a father.

# Chapter Five

Janet Booth was aged 43 when her life changed forever.

Visiting her grandmother, Getrude Batstone in Northamptonshire in 1985, she was with her husband Jim and her mother when the conversation turned to the family's history, something Janet was researching in her spare time.

Gertrude, now in her nineties, was living with her daughter Margie, the half-sister of her other daughter Gertie. Janet, who was planning a trip to France with her husband and their daughters Rachel and Lizzie, was keen to learn more about her grandfather, who she knew died on the Western Front in 1916. Up until that point she was led to believe that Harry had died in action like millions of others, and was buried alongside his comrades in Northern France, and so she asked her grandmother for the exact location so they could visit Harry's grave.

Recalling the scene, Janet said: 'There are certain precise moments in your life that you never forget, memories that remain etched on your mind forever; it was this statement that my Nan made while on one of my visits to her that I shall never forget. For a moment there was an awkward silence as she looked furtively towards my mum. The silence was broken by Nan, her voice shaking slightly.

'"Well", she said, almost whispering, "he doesn't actually have a grave, you see, she continued – he was executed in 1916. Harry, your grandfather, was shot for showing cowardice in the face of the enemy. The Army decided that due to the circumstances of his death he didn't deserve a proper grave. He had let his country down and was shot by a British firing squad; the men were from his own regiment – the West Yorkshires."'

For Janet, the revelation was as fascinating as it was dreadful and shocking, but for Gertrude, it was a moment of confessional release, and she spent the afternoon speaking of the man she loved so dearly and was taken from her in such brutal circumstances. But before she did, there was a silence between the three women, as Janet began to wonder why this information had been kept from her for so long.

It was broken by her mother, by then aged 71, who said that she too had only learned the truth about her father when she was in her forties. Gertie had been invited to a family gathering in the 1950s when her aunty Nellie, Harry's sister, came back to Britain from the U.S. where she had emigrated, first to take a job as a nanny before getting married. At the reunion, Nellie asked her brothers the truth about Harry's death, evidently she had been too young to know what happened to him. However the men would not divulge what had become a family secret, and told her they did not speak of it. But it later emerged that the brothers would raise a glass to Harry every Armistice Day, their own way of remembering a brother whose loss had been turned into a dark family secret.

Gertie, who never knew her father having lost him when she was just three, went to visit her mother after the reunion, and asked her about her father. 'What's this Nellie said about my dad dying in suspicious circumstances?' she said.

'I might as well tell you the truth as it seems the story is now general knowledge,' replied Gertrude. 'Your dad was shot for cowardice during the First World War. I never ever told you before because what happened to your dad was so dreadful and so unbearable for me. The shame and the stigma attached to someone in the family being branded a coward was something I had to carry with me all my life. I felt all the blame was on my shoulders,' she said. 'It was such a long time ago and I have tried to bury all the sadness that I felt – I did not want you knowing how he died. I want you to know that your dad was no coward, he was suffering from shellshock at the time of his execution – he was a very sick man,' she added. Nowadays families might have begun to talk about such heart-rending matters in a bid to ease the pain suffered by generations. But this was post-war 1950s Britain, where every family had endured some form of heartache and loss in the decade before.

The family secret, which had been kept for more than 40 years, was to be repressed again until Janet's chance discovery in 1985. The news sparked a desire to learn more, and Janet embarked upon tracing her family tree, and noting down her recollections of Harry, his life, his service and what she knew of his untimely death. Once she began talking about her first love, Gertrude couldn't stop. It was as if a floodgate had opened, and all the hidden memories were revealed. Janet began to research the circumstances of her grandfather's death, but quickly found her investigations hampered by the official secrecy surrounding First World War executions.

Her interest waned until a friend with a keen interest in military history directed her to Anthony Babington's For The Sake of Example, enabling her to pinpoint Harry's case despite restrictions on the author meaning he could not name the executed men. Files such as Harry's had been classified and were not set to be released for 75 years from the date of his death. It meant Janet was unable to see his court martial papers until late 1991. After reading the papers she decided not to divulge the dreadful contents to her grandmother because she believed it would be too upsetting for her.

---

In 1992, Labour's Andrew Mackinlay had been an MP for just a few months when he launched an ambitious and controversial bid to pardon British soldiers shot by their own side for military offences during the First World War. His interest in the war was piqued as a child by his grandfather, a Ypres veteran wounded in service who died when the future MP was just four, but by then he had instilled in the youngster a great interest in the conflict which remained with him.

Another seminal experience came at the age of 14, when Mr Mackinlay visited his uncle, Frank Beanes, in Springfield Hospital, Tooting. Mr Beanes spent 40 years there before his death, apparently never speaking a word after a massive mental breakdown while on active service in India. Mr Beanes had joined the Lincolnshire Regiment after the First World War and was sent to Ireland to fight against the Republican movement.

In 1921 he was part of a patrol that was ambushed by the IRA, costing the lives of two of his comrades. Mr Beanes helped fight off the attack and was awarded a gallantry medal. But the action was to have a devastating impact on him. After returning on leave to Britain he was unable to locate his family in Neasden, north-west London, and was then shipped out to India where he suffered a massive, irretrievable nervous collapse.

Mr Mackinlay said: 'It means that I had a personal experience of post-traumatic stress, personal as in a loved-one and a feeling of loss because basically in that ambush of 1921 my family lost their brother and my uncle.' But the start of his campaign began in the months after Mr Mackinlay won his seat in the 1992 election, when he became the Labour MP for Thurrock in Essex.

Feeling burnt out after his victory and suffering from depression despite achieving his lifetime ambition of becoming an MP, Mr Mackinlay took a trip to Ypres with his wife and daughter, and they visited Tyne Cot cemetery where 11,956 Allied servicemen are buried, of whom 8,369 have not been identified.

It was here that Mr Mackinlay decided to pay his own small tribute to the 306 soldiers executed for military offences by putting down an Early Day Motion in the House of Commons. He said: 'I remember we were looking for one particular grave up there (of an executed soldier) and I thought I'm now a Member of Parliament, I can make my little memorial, my little gesture to these soldiers by putting down an Early Day Motion. (EDM)'

Early Day Motions are a way of an MP raising an issue important to them or their constituents by submitting formal motions for debate. Though they rarely make it to the chamber for debate, fellow MPs are able to show their support by signing an EDM. Describing such a move as 'parliamentary graffiti', Mr Mackinlay later said he didn't expect it to go anywhere, but fellow MPs took notice and 67 signed the motion submitted in June 1992, meaning more than 10 per cent of all 651 MPs signed it. They included fellow Labour MPs Tony Banks, Frank Field and future Secretary of State for Defence Geoff Hoon. Support also came across the political divide, from all parties including the Lib Dems, Plaid Cymru, the Scottish National Party and even the Conservatives, in the form of ex-minister Peter Bottomley.

Mr Mackinlay called on the House to acknowledge that it was 'not too late to restore the names and reputations of the 306 soldiers of the British Empire Forces court martialled and executed, mostly on the Western Front in the four years 1914-18'. He pointed to 'deficiencies' in the court process and also to the official change in attitude towards troops who were guilty of military offences, pointing to the fact that no British soldiers were executed for such offences during the Second World War. Concluding the motion, he said: 'Compassion and justice dictates that all of these soldiers should now be treated as victims of the conflict and urges the Prime Minister to recommend a posthumous pardon for all 306, thus bringing to a close deeply unhappy and controversial chapter in the history of the Great War.'

Mr Mackinlay was beginning his campaign in the spirit of the late Ernest Thurtle, a Labour MP who helped bring about the abolition of the death penalty for military offences, in 1930. Mr Thurtle fought in the First World War and was seriously injured at the Battle of Cambrai in 1917. He entered parliament as the MP for Shoreditch, London, in 1923 and his high-profile campaigning pushed the issue to the forefront of the political agenda by the time Labour was elected in the General Election of 1929.

He was not alone in his concerns about the disciplinary system that existed during the First World War – disquiet about it had led to the formation of the Darling Committee in 1919. Under chairman Sir Charles Darling, the committee was to investigate 'the laws and rules of procedure regulating military courts martial'.[113]

After 22 days of evidence, it produced conflicting conclusions, with a majority and a minority report, the latter authored by three MPs, being published. The majority report, on the whole, found that the courts martial had been 'well done' during the conflict. Yet in the minority report there were concerns about the inexperience in military law of officers who sat in judgment on those accused of military offences. The fact that there was no right to an appeal in death penalty cases was a major issue and one of the MPs sought to amend this in Parliament but it was voted down in 1920.

In 1920 the Southborough Committee was set up to look specifically at shell-shock during the war. Under the chairmanship of Lord Southborough the 'Shell-Shock Committee' heard evidence from 59 witnesses over a two-year period. It concluded that the terms 'shell-shock' was misleading, equating hysteria and psychological problems suffered by soldiers to conditions suffered in normal life, and made an attempt to move away from the physical link to high explosive that had earlier dominated the debate.

Its most important findings concerned self-control and cowardice and the paradox of that situation – if he is capable of controlling his fear but acts as a coward he is guilty of a military offence, but if he is incapable of controlling himself he is not. In its report, the committee said: 'It is here that the difficulty arises in cases of war neurosis for it becomes necessary to decide whether the individual has or has not crossed that indefinite line which divides normal reaction from neurosis with impairment of volitional control.'[114]

However, this problematic description of defining cowardice would much later become to be seen as an example of how wrongly the authorities handled the matter during the war. Chris Walsh, in his book Cowardice – A Brief History said: 'Opponents of the cowardly label can argue that the logic of cowardice is brutal and barbaric. When it comes to judging alleged cowards, "those who are unable to control fear and so shrink from danger or trouble," as the dictionary puts it, should not be judged morally but instead helped therapeutically.

'By definition they are "unable" – *they cannot help it*. Cowardice is a misunderstood condition of some kind, often an understandably adverse reaction to trauma. The coward in this light is a victim being crushed by authority, the state and his peers. The very idea of cowardice is one of his victimisers.'[115]

The committee's recommendations for future conflicts was for a more rigorous recruitment policy, ensuring men who were pre-disposed to such problems were not sent to fight. But it underlined the school of thought that cases of mental breakdown, whatever the circumstance, should not be classified as battle casualties. Indeed, its conclusions suggested that shell-shock was completely avoidable, and that poor morale was an underlying cause of such cases.[116]

Against this backdrop of authorities effectively justifying the at times rough justice of the First World War, Mr Thurtle wrote a pamphlet entitled Shootings At Dawn – The Army Death Penalty at Work. In it, he recounted anonymous letters from soldiers who supported his call the end battlefield executions.

It even contained a letter from a soldier of the First Battalion, West Yorkshire Regiment, who recalled how on February 9, 1916, 'I was ordered to take over the guard of Lance-Corporal "X", of the same regiment, who was to be shot for desertion, having been absent for 23 days, until apprehended by the police. He was not shot until two days after this. On the evening of the 10th I handed him over to the new guard and proceeded with my platoon to the trenches. The next day I was ordered to pick the two worst characters in my platoon to form part of the execution party. "X" was a clean, smart brave soldier respected by all his comrades.

'The two men I selected for the firing party went with the adjutant. When they came back, tough characters though they were supposed to be, they were sick, they screamed in their sleep, they vomited immediately after eating. All they could say was: "The sight was horrible, made more so by the fact we had shot one of our own men."'

The same letter writer said that just a week later, he was tasked with assembling a firing party for another man destined to die after being found guilty of desertion. Picking 12 men from a cohort of prisoners who were being held for minor offences, he was shocked by their reactions to his unenviable task. He said: 'Men I had known for years as clean, decent, self-respecting soldiers, whose only offence was an occasional military "drunk," screamed out, begging not to be made into murderers. They offered me all they had if I would not take them for the job.'[117]

Mr Thurtle himself wrote with barely disguised anger about the executions. He said: 'In these days, no democracy has the right to shoot any man in cold blood, volunteer or conscript, because he is unable to stand the horrors of modern war. If war cannot be waged without the death penalty, and we take that penalty away, so much worse for the people who make wars but take good care not to fight them.'[118]

As well as parliamentarians, Mr Mackinlay's motion also caught the attention of the media, with several articles and television items about the new MP's bid for official recognition for the executed men. It was around this time that Janet received a telephone call from her grandmother Gertrude. She said: 'I was surprised to hear from her as she very rarely rang me, but this particular evening she sounded very excited. She had just seen the newly appointed Labour MP Andrew Mackinlay on the television stating that he was going to campaign for the executed soldiers of the First World War to be pardoned.

'Mr Mackinlay believed that the majority of men had not been given a fair trial at their courts martial. Many of the men at the time of their arrest had been suffering shellshock or battle fatigue. My Gran encouraged me to write to Mr Mackinlay to inform him that she was the widow of Private Harry Farr.'

The letter was sent in June 1992 and Janet said: 'My grandmother is still alive at 98. Although very frail now her mind is sharp. She told me how she felt when she received the letter from the War Office telling her her husband had been shot as a coward, and therefore she would not receive a widow's pension because of his cowardice. My greatest wish would be to hand my grandmother that piece of paper granting my grandfather's pardon.'

However, in his excitement at receiving such a letter and a tangible link with the executed soldiers, the MP mislaid it, much to his anxiety. He said: 'Fortunately she wrote to me again and I think in a sense it was divine providence because if we wanted a quintessential or iconic person for the campaign, the tragic case of Harry Farr is clearly the best one because his case is so well-documented.

'Documented to the extent that it shows that he had suffered shell-shock, it is not a matter for debate, it is acknowledged by the authorities that he had shell-shock and it's all in the court martial papers. The importance of [the] Harry Farr [case] was it rebutted the excuse put forward by a number of people including John Major, Viscount Cranborne, a junior defence Minister and others that it was a matter of history, as if it was such a long distance past. It wasn't history because unfortunately for those people who wanted to stop me in my campaign his widow was still alive. Very much alive, physically frail but with all her faculties at 99 years of age.'

In November 1992 Mr Mackinlay replied to Janet. In his letter, he said: 'I cannot overstate how pleased I am to have been able to make contact with you and to learn your grandmother is still alive and resolved, with us, to get Harry Farr exonerated, albeit three-quarters of a century late!'

In early summer 1993 Mr Mackinlay met Gertrude and her daughter, Gertie, at her home in Raunds, Northamptonshire, in the company of historian Julian Putkowski, who was to become a leading figure in the Shot At Dawn campaign group.

The group's conversation was recorded by Mr Putkowski with Janet's permission, unbeknown to Gertrude who spoke freely about her husband's story.

Mr Putkowski was an academic and author who jointly wrote Shot At Dawn with Julian Sykes, published in 1989. The book was an attempt to document the cases of all the soldiers and sailors who were executed for military offences. Over the course of several years the authors pieced together the histories of those first revealed by Anthony Babington in his 1985 book For The Sake Of Example.

Mr Putkowski and Mr Sykes first made contact via letter sent to the Imperial War Museum when the latter learned of Mr Putkowski's PhD research into British Army mutinies in the First World War. Beginning jointly in about 1981, the pair decided to embark on a project to identify all of those who were shot by their own side. Mr Putkowski said: 'He (Mr Sykes) had been working on it for 11 years altogether, I took eight years, we overlapped obviously. Until we had just about the lot. We were helped by Judge Anthony Babington who brought out his book For The Sake of Example.

'He had been allowed to look at the files which nobody else had but he was a crafty old dog, although he was a judge and the pillar of respectability and also Conservative, he was also Christian and had quite a conscience about what he saw were miscarriages of justice. The MoD put as a condition, no disclosure of names, no direct quotes from the documents so it was all in reported speech and he had to redact the names but he was allowed to put the letter, the first letter of the surnames. We were still missing about half a dozen, we spotted them all thanks to him.'

According to Mr Putkowski, the book made few ripples but established him as a leading figure in this relatively untouched field of First World War military discipline. Its publication also led to Mr Mackinlay contacting Mr Putkowski to see if they could work on a campaign together.

Mr Putkowski said: 'I had never heard of Andrew Mackinlay, I had to look up where Thurrock was even though I live in London, I had no connection whatsoever. I got a message through the publisher, I think it was a phone call or a letter, would I come down and meet him, and I think I went down to the House of Commons. He said I've read your book. He was very earnest... when I met him he was full of energy and that was going to make his mark. He said we'll do lots of things for the party and Labour Party policy and so on but this is a personal one. So I had a long chat about it and I said I'd support him.'

But before Janet Booth and Mr Putkowski came on board with Mr Mackinlay, the initial official response to his campaign and correspondence with Downing Street was not promising. In a letter dated July 16 1992, John Major said that he did not wish to pass judgment on any soldiers involved in the First World War – either those on trial by court martial or the men administering military justice. He also claimed that files held by the MoD on those who were executed did not contain enough information on their health to draw conclusions on their state of mind. He said: 'We are able to learn from history and the experiences of earlier generations, but I think it would be wrong to try and rewrite the events of the past to accord with modern philosophies and outlooks.' The tone and arguments made in the letter were to become all-too-familiar with campaigners who experienced many such responses over the next 14 years.

Interest in the burgeoning campaign peaked again in the run up to Remembrance Sunday in 1992. Mt Mackinlay also noticed a surge of interest from schools, with requests for help on documents and information about the campaign. He said: 'I actually do believe this opened up a whole interest in World War One. It was multi-curricular because it had history, geography, social policy and teachers love it. If you are talking about the Von Schliffen plan, kids' eyes blur over. But there is a photograph and there's pictures in the local press. And schools now go increasingly to Flanders and they look for the graves of a soldier executed in World War One, they've got Julian's list. We were sending out stuff as much as we could, photocopies of stuff, photocopies of my bill wherever we could do it. We were overwhelmed.'

One former Prime Minister did put his name forward publically by signing an Early Day Motion. Edward Heath was Conservative MP for Old Bexley and Sidcup, Father of the House and a former Royal Artillery officer who was mentioned in despatches in 1944 for his service during action in Europe.[119] After submitting his motion complete with signatures of supporters, staff at the Table Office, adept at identifying the various scrawls of the parliamentarians, were faced with one they had never seen before. Mr Mackinlay had to insist it was Mr Heath's but the incredulous staff decided to call his office to check, who also said they wouldn't have thought it was the case. But later his office confirmed that he was supporting the motion, a small but significant victory for Mr Mackinlay.

In November 1992 Mrs Booth, on the advice of Mr Putkowski, wrote to the Ministry of Defence to request enlistment papers, medical records and service records of Harry, enclosing proof that she and her mother were related to him. Perhaps unsurprisingly due to the sensitive nature of the information contained in the documents, no disclosure was made. However, the MoD did reply promptly and suggested that the records no longer existed.

In a letter from an official at the Army Records Centre in Hayes, West London, it says: 'I am sorry to say … that we have no documents relating to Private Farr. In 1940, during the London Blitz, an enemy incendiary device caused great damage to a huge collection of War Office records and around 60 per cent of the records of soldiers who fought in World War One were totally destroyed. Evidently those of Private Farr were among them.'

This was followed in the new year by further disappointing news from Number 10, in the form of a letter that sought to end the matter. In it, Mr Major outlined the results of a study of a sample 30 records - about 10 per cent of the 306 – that he had instructed junior defence minister Robert Cranborne to examine.

The Prime Minister said: 'It seems to me there are two main grounds on which pardons might be recommended. The first is that of legal impropriety of the error. The files record each stage of the case, up to the final decision by the Commander-in-Chief. No evidence was found to lead us, including the Judge Advocate General, to think that the convictions were unsound or that the accused were treated unfairly at the time.

'The second ground is humanitarian. I accept that this is a much more difficult area. I appreciate the distress which surviving relatives of the soldiers, such as Mrs Farr, still feel and I greatly sympathise with them. I do think it is essential, however, that full account is taken of the circumstances of the time.' He went on to point to the horrific casualties sustained in the First World War, and the impact on discipline if desertion was not treated as a capital offence.

The Prime Minister continued: 'As to shell-shock and the states of mind of the soldiers concerned, medical evidence is not always available on each file and, in many cases, was not a factor in the soldiers' plea of mitigation. However, shell-shock did become recognised as a medical condition during the First World War. And where medical evidence was available to the court, it was taken into account in sentencing and in the recommendations of the final sentence made to the Commander-in-Chief. Most death sentences were commuted on the basis of medical evidence.'

The conclusion of the letter is bleak and seeks to end the matter once and for all. Mr Major said: 'I have reached the conclusion that we cannot re-write history by substituting out latter-day judgment for that of contemporaries, whatever we might think. With the passage of time, attitudes and values change. I am sure that all people, when they think of this subject now, recognise that those soldiers who deserted did so in the most appalling conditions and under the most terrible pressure and take that fully into account in reaching any judgment in their own mind.'

He ends the letter by apologising for the 'deeply disappointing' response but goes on to assure Mr Mackinlay that he had not made the decision lightly. Despite the hopes of Mr Major, this was not the end of the matter, as just nine days later Mr Mackinlay organised a press conference in which he handed copies of the three-page letter to journalists.

In the meantime, the MP responded to Mr Major informing him that he disagreed with his decision not to pursue the matter further. In his letter, he said: 'I cannot agree with your contention that the accused were treated fairly at the time. At an elementary level, for example, the accused should have been advised they had the right to lodge a personal appeal for a pardon from H.M. the King. There is no evidence to show they were so informed.'

Citing the 'harrowing emotional effect' on Private Farr's family and pointing to the fact that it was acknowledged that he had suffered from shell-shock but was executed anyway, he urged the Prime Minister to reconsider. It was at this stage Janet was to step into the media spotlight for the first time, introduced to journalists as the granddaughter of Harry Farr and his still-living widow, whom she represented.

She joined Mr Mackinlay and Mr Putkowski on February 19 1993 in Westminster Hall for the meeting with reporters and photographers.

For the men, it was an important day, but attending a press conference was not unusual to them. For Janet it was the moment when she stepped into the limelight, was no longer merely corresponding with an MP but becoming a key member of the campaign, representing her mother, her grandmother and of course Harry.

Mr Mackinlay said: 'She'd never done anything like it before. People like myself we tend to take this for granted, this was both a brave step and an important step in her life and that of her mother and she has been a remarkable woman.'

Mr Putkowski said that the press conference marked the moment that Janet began her journey to national prominence regarding the campaign. He said: 'She was the go-to person. I'm not sure if she had the time but she made the time. Gertrude before she went into the care home did a few interviews but she was quite frail. There were some signature interviews but they were always quite short and she never quite had the delivery that Janet got. Janet was much, much more driven. She also had the benefit of context.'

For Janet it was a daunting yet exciting day, in which she spoke extensively about the discovery of her family's dark secret, its impact upon the lives of her mother and grandmother and her hopes for a pardon for Harry. Yet she recalls thinking to herself: 'What am I doing here? I know nothing really, apart from how he died.'

Speaking of Gertrude, now 98, she said: 'She has lived with the shame and humiliation all these years. A pardon would mean she could rest in peace. The whole family is angry.'[120] Mr Putkowski, alongside her, said: 'The court martial said Harry Farr tried to escape but in fact he just fell apart in a nervous collapse. He had been in hospital for five months from a previous collapse and should have never been returned.'[121]

The response from the public was immediate and seemingly whole-heartedly in support of the campaign and in particular the Farr family. One letter, from a soldier's wife in Shaftesbury, Dorset, said: 'We feel intense sympathy for you and do support you and your family in efforts to have the decision reversed.' Another First World War enthusiast wrote: 'Private Farr was no criminal. He, I believe, deserves the pardon that you asked for.' A teacher at a school in Essex also wrote to explain the impact of the campaign on pupils and said some had written to both John Major and the MoD to plead the case for a pardon. He also asked permission to show children copies of the court martial documents which he had been given by Mr Mackinlay, to which Mrs Booth assented.

Second World War veteran Ivor Watkins, whose father served in the First World War, added his name to the growing list of support to the campaign. In a letter, he wrote: 'Your grandfather, like us, never asked to fight his fellow man and was pulled into a conflict through the failings of those who governed and should have known better. I knew many veterans of the Great War and I am sure that, to a man, they would have been equally saddened and aggrieved at his treatment.'

The press conference piqued the interest of local and national press across Britain. Regional evening papers carried the story the same day, and that in turn led to some readers wondering how they could become part of the newly founded campaign. Mr Mackinlay said: 'The generals managed to execute somebody from every corner of the United Kingdom so there was almost somebody from every regional newsroom and so many local papers had stories.'

In the north-east of England, a man called John Hipkin read about the plight of the executed men and Mr Mackinlay's passionate determination to right the perceived wrongs of that age. Mr Hipkin had a strong sense of natural justice and an incredible early life story. In 1941, aged just 14, Mr Hipkin joined the merchant navy and went to sea as a cabin boy on the tanker SS Lustrous, which was headed to the West Indies. After just 21 days at sea off Newfoundland, the tanker was sunk by a German warship but all hands survived and were taken back to Europe where Mr Hipkin became the youngest British prisoner of war. The boy sailor was taken with his comrades to Stalag XB near Hamburg in Germany where he was to remain until it was liberated by British forces in April 1945.[122]

Mr Putkowski said: 'John Hipkin utterly and completely independently – no connection with us at all, I think he wrote to Andrew Mckinlay - … started off on his own autonomous campaign.' His tenacity and dedication to the cause was to become legendary among campaigners, and his regular newsletter updates helped bind the supporters together.

## Chapter Six

In 1929, the death penalty for military offences was removed from the statutes, something Mr Mackinlay believes is indicative of the shame felt by politicians in the aftermath of the slaughter of the Great War. He said: 'My view is frankly the establishment felt ashamed, what happened to these men. I can't prove that but that's my reading and judgment. There was an awful lot of disquiet in Parliament about it. Also there were many people who were in World War One and it left bitter memories.'
He pointed to a letter sent to him by a woman whose father had survived the war, but was angered by the prospect of a memorial to Black Watch soldiers killed in the First World War would not contain the names of those shot for cowardice, desertion or similar offences. Mr Mackinlay said: 'They let it be known to the authorities – that was the phrase used – that if the monument went up without the names, the monument wasn't going to stand. She told me her father actually had explosives in his shed, with the intention of blowing it up. It certainly wasn't blown up and as far as I'm aware their names went on the war memorial.'
As a traditional Labour MP, the part played by class in the execution of soldiers by Britain was not insignificant to Mr Mackinlay. He pointed to the fact that just three officers were executed in the First World War, while 303 men faced the firing squad.
Second Lieutenant Eric Skeffington Poole was the first officer executed in the First World War, despite a history of suffering from shell-shock. Having applied for a commission, he became a second lieutenant in the 11th Battalion, West Yorkshire Regiment, the same regiment as Harry. In October 1916 he was fighting in the Somme region, he went missing for two days when his platoon was due to relieve soldiers in the front line, and was subsequently charged with desertion.

Initial inquiries showed he had suffered from shell-shock in July of that year and a medical examination by a Royal Army Medical Corps officer found he was in good health but had a 'high-strung, neurotic temperament'. Like Harry, a medical board was not convened before the trial to examine him and shell-shock was not a simple defence at this time. He was later examined by such a board, but its president was an officer who had previously returned him to the front marked fit for service after the shell-shock incident. Despite senior officers calling for leniency, he was executed at Poperinghe on December 10 1916. He died aged 31, and the nature of his death proved an overwhelming source of shame for his family.

Sub Lieutenant Edwin Dyett was the second officer to be executed for a military offence during the Frist World War. A Royal Navy officer and son of a Merchant Navy captain, he served with the service's 63rd infantry division, fighting in the Somme region in the aftermath of the bloody summer battle of 1916. In November, the division was called upon to make a final attack before the winter proper, and Dyett was held in reserve as a spare officer. But as the casualties mounted in the wake of the rush towards German trenches, Dyett and another officer were sent forward and ordered to rejoin their battalion. However on the way they met another sub lieutenant who ordered them to take stragglers to the front, they argued and Dyett left claiming he would look for the battalion HQ for orders. But he was arrested, court martialled, found guilty of failing to join his battalion when ordered to and was executed on January 5 1917. He was aged 21. The death sentence handed down by the court was recommended to be commuted because of his age, lack of experience and the difficult conditions. However, General Gough, disagreed, writing: 'If a private had behaved as he did in such circumstances, it is highly probable that he would have been shot.'[123]

The final officer to be executed was Second Lieutenant John Paterson. He was shot by firing squad in September 1918, weeks before the end of the war. He was a deserter, having left his battalion in the Essex Regiment at the front and disappearing for a number of months. When confronted by military policemen, he shot one dead, leading to a murder conviction. Paterson was sentenced to death for both murder and the offence of desertion.

Mr Mackinlay said: 'Three officers were executed and those three officers were not of the upper crust, they were by the nature of war frankly middle-class folk [who] were made officers. But the establishment area, none of those were executed. Frankly I don't believe there weren't officers who cracked up, who were guilty of cowardice – not guilty in my eyes – who had they been non-commissioned ranks would have been court-martialled and executed. It didn't happen. It is a class thing here.'

Indeed, there were documented instances of officers causing severe disciplinary problems without suffering the ultimate sanction. Another battalion of the West Yorkshire Regiment, the Twelfth, witnessed such a situation during the Battle of Loos in September 1915. The regiment was tasting trench warfare for the first time and had suffered severe losses and had already heard of rumours of a general retreat when its officers and men were resting behind the front line.

An officer recorded: 'The men were utterly exhausted, and were still lying out in the pouring rain, when, in darkness, a mounted officer in British uniform (not of the West Yorkshire Regiment) galloped through the area calling out "The whole army is in full retreat, every man for himself". This officer was pulled off his horse before any serious effect had been produced. It appeared to be a case of advanced hysteria.'

Despite receiving letters he describes as 'flak' from opponents of his campaign, Mr Mackinlay quickly garnered public support and was heartened by the encouragement from colleagues and political heavyweights. He soon received a telephone call from Lord Houghton of Sowerby, a former minister who served in Howard Wilson's government and a First World War veteran who survived the Battle of the Somme when he was a teenage private soldier.[124]

When he spoke to Mr Mackinlay, he was well into his 90s and had previously spoken repeatedly about his experience of the horror of the Somme and other battles. Mr Mackinlay said: 'He said "I've just phoned you up to say well done and keep at it" and I let him talk and he said "after all this goes to the heart of our Christian principles. "Forgiveness, forgiveness." He repeated it. And then he paused and then he said: "That's wrong. It's not a matter for forgiveness. These people did nothing wrong. They were honourable, decent, brave men." And he broke down. He broke down on the end of the phone. I surmised from this he had been witness to or privy to an execution as indeed many people would have done and as indeed many people wrote to me.'

Mr Mackinlay said he received many letters from the children of First World War veterans, saying that they would never speak of their service. But some were linked by a recurring theme, that towards the end of their lives, some of these men broke down in front of their families and spoke of either taking part in or witnessing firing squads, executing men convicted of offences such as cowardice.

The MP also received letters of support from current and past NCOs, supporting his work. He received notes from veterans of both wars as well as more recent and even current personnel. He said: 'At the time they were all non-commissioned officers, warrant officers, the equivalent in the RAF, Royal Marine Regimental Sergeant Majors. And these were guys who were not on the left, they would be Daily Mail readers, that's where they would be.'

However, there was opposition too. The Royal British Legion did not initially support the campaign, something Mr Mackinlay believes was a result of its leadership being nervous about the reaction of its members. Yet at its annual conference in 1985, two years after the publication of Babington's For The Sake of Example, British Legion members voted to 'urge the Government to re-open all "verdicts of guilt" cases for acts of cowardice in the First World War in the light of modern medical evidence.'[125] Unfortunately, after being told by the Ministry of Defence that the records to assist the exoneration of the executed soldiers may not exist, the Legion's council decided 'that no useful purpose would be served by pursuing this issue'.

On April 27, the Prime Minister again replied to Mr Mackinlay addressing his latest plea for a pardon. He said: 'I fully recognise the feelings of the Farr family and others in a similar situation. Indeed that has made this decision all the more difficult. I respect your deep concern on this issue. I am afraid, however, that we must continue to agree to disagree.'

But Mr Mackinlay refused again to take no for an answer and wrote once more to the Prime Minister in May 1993. He said that though he had no wish to rewrite history, the issue was current for the first time since the First World War because the information relating to the courts martial had been classified until now. He went on: 'I do not primarily view this matter as simply a debate about the alteration or amendment of history. It is a contemporary humanitarian issue for at least as long as Harry Farr's widow remains alive.'

He urged Mr Major to re-read the court martial document relating to Harry's trial and requested him to hold a meeting with Harry's widow: 'Although she is a physically frail 99-year-old, she retains all her faculties and continues to suffer abiding pain and distress about the injustice meted out to her husband, her daughter and herself. It is, of course, late in the day, in more than one sense – but both you and I have an obligation to consider this request from a person whose remaining years must be desperately few.'

In the letter, the MP also formally requested the return of documents given to the Earl of Clarendon in mid-1917 by Mrs Farr. But Mr Major was adamant that no such pardon should occur, not even in the singular case of Private Farr. He said in a letter dated June 14 1993: 'To grant a pardon on humanitarian grounds would result in the ring-fencing of an individual case to the deep disappointment and anguish of family and relatives.' Further disappointing news was Mr Major's assurance that the documents could not be found in any archive. However, his letter contained words of encouragement and in the view of Mr MacKinlay, decent sentiment and respect for his campaign and those who had paid the ultimate price.

For Gertrude Batstone, Mr Major's letter proved to be the final chapter in her quest to clear her late husband's name. She died on July 22 aged 99, in Raunds, Northamptonshire, leaving behind four generations of children and grandchildren. At her funeral, the story of Harry's sad demise was not repeated, but in a eulogy read by a local vicar he was mentioned as her first husband.

In a letter of condolence, Mr Mackinlay referred to the Sermon on the Mount, writing: 'Those who have struggled, endured their adversity, suffered hardness and persecution in this life "shall have their rich reward in heaven". I do believe that and in particular in relation to Gertrude Batstone.'

At this stage, the Press coverage of Gertrude's death generated a new wave of general media interest, with requests for interviews from documentary-makers, showing that a more in-depth interest in the campaign was growing. In the summer, the efforts to achieve a pardon hit another setback, this time with the revelation that the Ministry of Defence had thrown away thousands of relevant files that could have been used to help secure pardons.

During the First World War, more than 3,000 British and Commonwealth soldiers were sentenced to death for military offences, but only 306 executions were carried out. More than 2,700 soldiers were spared, their sentences commuted by the higher echelons of the Armed Services. And yet, the Ministry of Defence when questioned in August 1993 on the whereabouts of the files relating to their cases, could only say that they had been disposed of before 1947 because they were 'no longer required for administrative use'[126]

Such files could have thrown light on the arbitrary use of field executions – proof that cases genuinely deserving of the death penalty led to the survival of the individual, which could be compared with cases such of that of Harry, who clearly should not have been shot at dawn. Mr Mackinlay described the revelation as outrageous. He said: 'Unfortunately whoever made the decision isn't around anymore, but it's convenient, isn't it? It makes it much more difficult to examine whether the men executed were judged fairly by the standards of the time.'[127]

Mr Putkowski began to help the MP with his correspondence regarding the campaign, becoming an unofficial, unpaid researcher. He said: 'I was like a parliamentary researcher but nothing to do with parliament. This was Andrew's pet individual project and that was OK by me.

'I started dealing at first with the correspondence. I had an idea that we'd get tons and tons of stories but we didn't. Enormous numbers of people writing "right on. I really believe this was a terrible business" but actually there wasn't much more to capitalise on than what was in the book.'

BBC Radio 4 produced a documentary featuring an interview with Gertrude called It Is With Regret. It was aired on September 16 and featured audio footage obtained by Mr Putkowski earlier in the summer. The introduction to the story began with Gertrude's voice, saying: 'He was no coward. A finer soldier never lived'.

She said: 'Some nights he'd come along the square, we were in St. Charles Square where I lived, he'd come along and give a whistle and I'd look out the kitchen window and see him on the opposite side and I would say to the lady could I please go and post a letter. I didn't want to post a letter, I was a naughty girl, just to see him. I used to run down in my cap and apron just to say hello and have a word with him and come back.'

Interviewer: 'What did he look like?'

Gertrude: 'Very smart and very good-looking. Very curly hair he had.'

Interviewer: 'What colour eyes did he have?'

Gertrude: 'Green eyes they called them on his Army papers, they were supposed to be green but they were more a deep grey.

'He was four years older than me and I know my mother and my sisters, they all grumbled. They said at the time "he's too old for you, he's too many years older, you shouldn't have him". They grumbled at the time, that's how I remember it so well but I remember as we all say "I love him, I'm going with him and that's that".'

Speaking of learning of Harry's death, she said: 'They just sent me a letter, a letter from the War Office, and all it said was: "Dear madam, we regret to inform you that your husband has died. He was sentenced for cowardice and was shot at dawn on the 18th of October 1916." They were the exact words. That was all I got.'

Interviewer: 'What did you do?'

Gertrude: 'What did I do? I got hold of that letter and I had a blouse on at that time and I pushed it right down in my blouse, so petrified I was in case anybody saw it and nobody did see it. I didn't want nobody to know what had happened. Nobody knew, I wouldn't tell anybody. I don't know, I thought it was so terrible I suppose. I felt it was so awful, I felt it was on my shoulders, all that stigma.

'That's how I felt. My dear mother didn't know, nor his mother, not until the time when my pension was stopped. Then I had to tell them because they wanted to know why I was ill and upset, then I had to tell them. That was the first time anybody knew, except myself.'

The documentary also used an actor to read out Mr Major's refusal letter in a voice sounding remarkably like his. Sue Gaisford, reviewing the programme for the Independent on Sunday under the headline Dear Mr Major, I Hope You Heard This, described the letter as 'reasonable, measured and deeply patronising'.

She said: 'It was not convincing. Perhaps, as General Farrar-Hockley said, such executions were a necessary deterrent, but Matt Thompson's finely constructed, compelling programme left its hearers persuaded that they were an appalling injustice.'[128]

In October 1993 Janet and her husband Jim visited Thiepval Memorial in the Somme region of France for the first time. Her grandfather Harry's name is one of 72,394 inscribed on the imposing 45m-high red-stone monument. All of the British and South African soldiers commemorated like Harry after being killed in the sector have no known grave and for families mourning loved-ones, Thiepval has become a place of pilgrimage.

Janet said: 'The awesome sight of the monument standing majestically against the stark countryside of the Somme remains with me to this day. Walking past the neatly tended row upon row of white crosses representing the graves of the men killed made me realise how many lives were lost during the First World War. So many wasted lives for so little ground gained. I felt quite emotional when I saw my grandfather's name carved on the wall of the monument. A strange feeling of tranquillity and stillness seemed to surround this small part of the Somme.'

A journalist from the BBC joined Janet on her trip to film scenes for an evening news report about the burgeoning campaign. It was to be the start of many television appearances by Janet in the coming years. Next was a request from Yorkshire Television to allow a television crew to accompany Janet on a trip to the Somme to pay tribute to her grandfather. An 18-minute long film was produced. This period also saw Janet appear on the BBC talk show Kilroy, in an episode entitled 'Defending Your Good Name'. Other television appearances included Sky News and Channel 4, where one producer was prompted to write: 'The best response we've had to a "comment" for a very long time.'

Newspaper journalists were also contacting Jane in this period and articles appeared in the Farnham Herald, Janet's local newspaper; the Express & Star in Wolverhampton, the Yorkshire Post and The Guardian.

The burgeoning national interest in the campaign was beginning to see small yet tangible results. In Durham Cathedral, the names of seven soldiers from the Durham Light Infantry who were executed during the First World War were added to the regiment's Book of Remembrance, which detailed 15,000 men who fell in the conflict. Major David Bowler, of the Durham Light Infantry Trust, said: 'It's not for us to pass judgment on what happened all those years ago. We don't have the power to pardon these men but once we realised they'd been excluded we felt they should at least be commemorated. After all, they died in the service of their country.'[129]

Between 1993 and 1995, Mr Mackinlay presented four bills with the intention of pardoning the soldiers and he succeeded in forcing debate on the subject. Because it was a matter of conscience, support was received from across the house – mostly from his fellow Labour MPs but consistent support also came from Tories such as Peter Bottomley. In October 1993, Mr Mackinlay introduced his bill, calling a press conference on October 12, a week before he stood in the Commons.

At the press conference in the Jubilee Room, Westminster Hall he once again sat alongside Janet Booth and Mr Putkowski. Janet spoke of her own personal journey of discovery about her family's hidden past and also of a moving pilgrimage she had made to the battlefields of northern France just a week before. Janet said: 'My grandfather had been at the front since 1914. He fought at Flanders. We found the place where we believe he refused to go over the top at the Somme on September 16, 1916 and we found the chateau where we think he had his court martial.'[130]

The first bill received its first reading on October 19 1993 as a 10 Minute Rule Bill – A Private Members' bill, which would provide 'a posthumous pardon for the 306 British and Empire soldiers executed in the Great War 1914-1918'. This type of bill allows backbench MPs to make their case in a short speech lasting for a maximum of 10 minutes. A speech opposing is also allowed, again lasting for a maximum of 10 minutes before the house decides whether to introduce the bill.[131]

Mr Mackinlay presented the 10-minute bill to the House of Commons, 'to pardon soldiers convicted of, and executed during the Great War of 1914 to 1919, for the offences of cowardice, desertion, sleeping at post, throwing away arms and striking a superior officer.' The bill was read for the first time and a second reading was ordered for the following month.

Addressing the requirements of the bill, he said it would apply to 306 soldiers of the British Empire Forces.[132] He said that many of those executed were young men, even teenagers and many were not conscripts but volunteers, drawn from every corner of the United Kingdom. He went on: 'Some spent not months but years in the trenches enduring constant shellfire, sniping and lack of food and sleep in the constant wet and cold. It is hardly surprising that in many cases, their spirits broke.'

He pointed to the fact that many of the guilty men were denied an opportunity to prepare a defence, were denied advocacy and those that were not represented by a legally qualified person. Mr Mackinlay claimed none of the soldiers and sailors were given the opportunity to appeal the sentence of death and many were given just 12-24 hours' notice before it was carried out. Describing the public record secrecy rule, which prevents publication of documents deemed potentially damaging for 30, 75 or even 100 years as 'crazy', he said that 'now the documents had been seen, it was plain to see that many of the men were sick, traumatised and suffering from shell-shock'. Explaining his motivation in bringing the bill, he said that the dependants of those men sought redress and claimed that the few thousand Great War veterans that were still alive would gain satisfaction that their comrades had been exonerated. He said that he had the support of Lord Houghton of Sowerby, a veteran of Passchendaele. 'It has been suggested that I am trying to re-write history – I reject that,' he said. 'I am seeking to ensure that history is written with clarity and precision and that those things that are uncomfortable to the establishment are brought into the open.'

He set out two options for the pardons of the soldiers – legislation to grant a blanket pardon for all 306 soldiers or a High Court judge-led case-by-case inquiry, sanctioned by the Secretary of State for Defence. The type of pardon was proposed to have the same effect as one made under Royal Prerogative – one that would not remove the soldiers' convictions but would 'nullify any degradations and penalties imposed'[133], i.e. the sentence of death.

Mr Mackinlay pointed to the groundswell of public opinion that had boosted his campaign since its inception 18 months earlier, saying the his postbag and those of fellow MPs were full, in support. He added: 'In a sense, the soldiers have already been pardoned by the highest court in the land – British public opinion.'

In response to the bill, Roger Evans, Conservative MP for Monmouth, rose to argue against the proposed pardons, using arguments that were to dog the campaign for years to come. Describing Mr Mackinlay's speech as 'plausible and emotional, but fundamentally misconceived and wrong in principle', he added: 'What are we hoping to achieve by this measure?' He said a blanket pardon 'will not be an examination of historical record, but a mere expression of opinion,' and added that the matter was for historians, not for the House.

However, the bill was ordered to be 'brought in' by Mr Mackinlay, with cross-party support from MPs including from Peter Bottomley (Conservative), Rev. Ian Paisley (Democratic Unionist), Alex Salmond (SNP) and Sir David Steel (Liberal Democrats).

In this instance, the bill was withdrawn and presented a day later, on November 3 1993 as a different type of bill. This time it was presented under Standing Order No 58[134], which at this time meant it was an ordinary presentation bill, as were two subsequent ones by Mr Mackinlay. Ordinary presentation bills are another type of Private Members' Bill but are introduced more formally, without speeches or opposition.[135] This bill, like two that followed did not make it to a second reading when MPs are given a chance to debate and vote on whether to allow it to proceed to the committee stage. This meant it had been timed out, with other parliamentary matters deemed more pressing taking precedent.

Initial indications from the Ministry of Defence to reporters suggested individual pardons were possible, but it opposed a blanket pardon due to the loss of records during the bombing of the Public Record Office at Hayes during the Second World War. But the attempt to pardon the soldiers gained praise from many quarters, including the pages of Private Eye magazine. Describing the initial refusal as 'heartless', the magazine said: 'There is little doubt that Mr Mackinlay's own bill – which he hopes to reintroduce in the next parliament – would become law given enough time and a free vote.'[136]

Throughout his time in parliament, Mr Mackinlay entered the ballot to be allowed to introduce a Private Members Bill concerning the pardons, but never won the chance. However, he persisted with bills that would be timed out, using the 10 Minute Rule.

It meant that at the very least he was able to make a speech on the matter. It also meant 150 copies of the bill were printed on official green House of Commons paper, which Mr Mackinlay would send to his supporters to thank them for their correspondence. And each year interest grew, with local papers returning to the same stories as Mr Mackinlay continued to ask questions in Parliament. He received some negative post in response, but characterised many of the authors as 'people who had to write on lined paper in capital letters with red pens'. In any case, it was a fraction of those heartfelt letters of support which spurred him on.

Janet meanwhile was working on obtaining signatures for a petition calling for pardons with the intention of presenting it in Parliament on July 1, marking the 78th anniversary of the start of the Battle of the Somme. A similar bill was presented in May 1994, with the first formal reading - without a speech – taking place on May 18, allowing 150 copies to be printed with the intention of supplying them to campaigners and supporters[137].

The day before, Mr Mackinlay wrote to Janet as he sat in a committee, stealing a moment to update her on the campaign. However, the strain of his new job was beginning to take its toll on him, and in a moment of confession he wrote: 'My lifestyle/pressures etc etc get worse and worse. John Smith's tragic and sad death is a lesson to us all here. I confess to being very very tired but it is not easy to get a break - even for a few hours. Alas I am rarely at home.'

A second reading of the bill took place on July 1, when Andrew Mackinlay presented a 25,000-signature petition in the House of Commons, mentioning that notable signatories included Janet Booth, Allan Harris (who is the nephew of Private Louis Harris of the West Yorkshire Regiment) and Grace Shoan, niece of Private Bertie McCubbin of the Sherwood Forresters.

Private Harris was shot four days before the end of the First World War on November 7, 1918 and was the last British soldier to be executed for a military offence. In September during an attack on German positions in Rocquigny, northern France, the 23-year-old Lewis gunner downed his kit and disappeared. He was charged with cowardice and an alternative charge of desertion, found guilty of the latter and despite not being represented at this late stage of the war, was sentenced to death.[138]

Private McCubbin was a volunteer and was fighting with the 17th Sherwood Forresters on the Somme during the July offensive in 1916. On the night he was arrested for cowardice, July 7, he had been in the trenches for 26 days continuously. He had disobeyed an order to proceed to a listening post 40 yards into No Man's Land and less than 200 yards from the enemy on a light night, complaining of internal pain. During his trial, he claimed to have suffered from nerves ever since a shell burst just three yards away, but he was found guilty, sentenced to death and shot by firing squad on July 30. Appallingly, his death certificate included the line: 'death was not instantaneous'.[139]

Mr Mackinlay said that the signatories wished to draw the House's attention to the soldiers of the British Empire who were executed by firing squad for offences including cowardice, desertion, disobedience, sleeping at post, throwing away arms and striking a superior officer. Addressing the House, Mr Mackinlay said: 'The petitioners believe that those men were denied fair trials in accordance with the rules of natural justice and note that documents now available prove that many were suffering from sickness and trauma.' He said that petitioners called for the House to introduce legislation to pardon the executed soldiers and that their names be added to all official records and war memorials. Again the bill was timed out.

On July 11, 1995 Mr Mackinlay's bill was presented for a third time and was ordered to be read for a second time three days later. However, it again failed to make the second reading stage, being timed out. But in September of that year, Gertie, Janet and Mr Mackinlay received a boost when it was reported that Labour leader Tony Blair was supporting the campaign.

The Times said that the executed soldiers could receive a posthumous pardon under a future Labour government, and illustrated the report with a picture of Janet, displaying family photos. In a letter to Mr Mackinlay, the leader's office said: 'While it would not be appropriate for Mr Blair to make a commitment at this stage, I can assure you that he is conscious of the wide-spread cross-party support for this matter to be reviewed, not only among members of Parliament but also throughout the country.' A spokesman for Mr Blair added: 'There is certainly a case for review.'[140]

On December 13 1995, the Armed Forces minister Nicholas Soames, grandson of Sir Winston Churchill, presented the Armed Forces Bill for its second reading. The Armed Forces Act must be renewed every five years, to allow the legal provision of a standing army in Britain. One of the bill's key issues was changes to the courts martial system of military discipline.

During its discussion, future Armed Forces minister and Labour MP Dr Reid spoke in his role as Mr Soames' shadow. After addressing a number of points about the bill including the proposal to allow guilty servicemen to appeal their sentence, in line with civilian courts, he called for consideration 'of past miscarriages of justice in the courts martial system, especially those that have affected large numbers of people'[141].

He mentioned Mr Mackinlay's campaign and a case that had affected his constituency – the Salerno Mutiny of the Second World War, the biggest in British wartime history. Members of the Tyne Tees (50th) and Highland (51st) divisions had thrown down their arms and refused to take part in the battle in September 1943. They were members of Montgomery's victorious 8th Army, and had been taken back to Africa from Italy for treatment of wounds, malaria and other illnesses.

Given the chance to re-join their units in Italy, many volunteered to leave, despite not being fully fit. However, as they crossed the Mediterranean, the men learned they were to be used as reinforcements in the US led campaign to gain a foothold in Northern Italy. The soldiers refused to fight, despite being threatened with the death penalty. The Army refused to back down, despite senior officers knowing that the men's transit was the result of an administrative error.

A total 191 men were arrested and taken back to North Africa for court martial. All were found guilty after a trial lasting just a week, with the defence given just six days to prepare for it. Sentences handed to the men were death penalties for three sergeants and between seven and 12 years' penal servitude for the rest. Only the intervention of Adjutant General Sir Ronald Adam led to the suspension of the sentences and the return of the men to their units. However, they were later stripped of their medals and given a reduced war pension after VE Day and faced accusations of cowardice for decades after.

Dr Reid said he brought up the pardons because of the case of John James MacFarlane, one of the so-called mutineers whose family were the MP's constituents. He said "through a mistake at best – let us hope it was not intentional – by his commanding officers, he and others were deprived of their medals, dishonoured, demeaned and dismissed. That is still deeply felt by that family in Hollyton in my constituency."

He went on: 'And the very least, we should not accept the bland dismissal of the right to rectify the miscarriages of justice merely because of the passing of time. That seems to be the position that has been accepted by the Prime Minister and the Government. Why it should be considered as an appropriate – indeed honourable course of action to rectify miscarriages, even posthumously, in civil society but not in military society is frankly beyond me. I would go further – the ability and will to recognise miscarriages of justice, even posthumously, reinforces the legitimacy of the justice system in the military'[142].

Later in the debate, Mr Mackinlay stood to speak about the pardons saying he wanted an amendment allowing them, either at the bill's committee or report stage. He again spoke of his belief that the executed men were denied natural justice and claimed the support of surviving veterans, as well as the British Legion. He said that the Prime Minister had written to him to express sympathy, but said 'there should be no pardons, because it is a matter for history'.

He pointed to the fact that although it was history, it was 'of our century' and that there was an immense interest in the subject among British schoolchildren. Because of this he said, there was a need for writing history with clarity and precision. Drawing Churchill into the debate, Mr Mackinlay referred to his doctor, Lord Moran, and his diaries and memoirs about shell-shock in the First World War. He also pointed to Judge Anthony Babington's For the Sake of Example and Shot At Dawn by Julian Putkowski and Julian Sykes as required reading.

Importantly, Mr Mackinlay called on the Prime Minister to consider a further route to the pardons, by asking the Queen to exercise Royal Prerogative, removing the need for legislation.[143]

Dr Reid responded first, by saying he believed it was never too late to right a wrong. He said: 'When people tell me, whether it be a private or the Prime Minister, that these things are merely matter of history, I commend to them Hegel's Maxim: "The owl of Minerva spreads its wings only at the coming of dusk".History is not a source of forgetting, it is ultimately the source of wisdom.'[144]

In response to Mr Mackinlay, Mr Soames said that after 'the most detailed and careful consideration' by the Prime Minister and the MoD, pardons had been ruled out. He said: 'The people executed – some 346 men [total includes murderers] – represented 11 per cent of the people condemned to death...

'A review found that there were no procedural errors or legal improprieties in the courts martial or in subsequent reviews by the chain of command. On those grounds, there is no basis for a pardon.' He went on: 'As a general principle it is inappropriate to reconsider historical events in the light of modern attitudes. Most soldiers stayed and fought in the trenches in appalling conditions, and they needed to be able to rely on their comrades.'[145]

The minister's words were a public pronouncement of what Mr Mackinlay was already aware through correspondence with the Prime Minister – that pardons would not be achieved while the Tories were in power or at the very least, while John Major remained in Downing Street.

However, undeterred by this apparent setback and buoyed by his party's apparently unassailable poll lead[146], Mr Mackinlay presented an amendment to the Armed Forces Bill on May 9 1996. It required the Defence Secretary to pardon the executed men or report to Parliament the reasons for not doing so in each case, within a year of the Act being passed.

Importantly, it contained the following clause: 'A pardon under this section shall not have any effect on any existing financial rights or obligations of any defendant.' It meant that any argument against the pardons on the basis it could prove costly and set a precedent in terms of retrospective compensation was blown away almost at the start. It also served to underline the moral and emotional drive behind the campaign to clear the men's names.

Mr Mackinlay's proposed pardons were referred to as 'new clause six'.[147] This clause did not require a tribunal to be involved, merely for the Secretary of State for Defence to either pardon the soldiers or submit an individual report explaining why a pardon was not appropriate. In setting out his proposal, Mr Mackinlay returned to his well-trodden arguments on a lack of natural justice, a lack of proper representation at trial and how many of those convicted were clearly sick, and the need to set the record straight.

For the first time in the chamber, Mr Mackinlay spoke in detail about Harry Farr's life, conviction and death. He said: 'I had the privilege of meeting his widow, Gertrude Batstone – she married again – in her 99th year. Throughout her long life, that wonderful woman sought recognition for her husband as a brave soldier, a volunteer who endured the trauma of the trenches not just for two months but for two years or more.

'After being shelled, he simply could not go on. He was hospitalised, but was forced to return to the front, and when he was told to go forward, he broke away from his escorts trembling. The "trembling" is documented in the field court martial records. Despite that, that poor man and many like him had to face a firing squad at dawn.'[148]

In response, John Wilkinson, Conservative MP for Ruislip-Northwood, said he disagreed with the amendment and sought to excuse the executions on disciplinary grounds. Similar arguments have been made since. In his book Mud, Blood and Poppycock, Gordon Corrigan explains that 'military justice is not just punitive, it is exemplary.'

He suggests that the Commander in Chief, when deciding whether or not to confirm a death sentence, had to look at the general situation that the soldier's unit was facing. 'He was entitled – indeed he was required – to consider the unit's state of discipline at the time and whether or not the offence was prevalent.'[149]

Mr Wilkinson said: 'How can [exonerate the dead] without a full appreciation of the circumstances – and without a full realisation that examples had to be made, and perhaps on occasion martyrs had to be made, to ensure the discipline and cohesion of whole units?'[150] Several MPs speaking after Mr Wilkinson condemned his speech, with Labour's Dr Goodman describing his comments as 'disgraceful'[151].

Dr Reid again came out in support of the pardons, saying: 'The idea that serving British soldiers should be shot "pour encourager les autres" is anathema to British tradition and it should stay that way.'[152] When the division bell sounded, Dr Reid joined Mr Mackinlay and 127 others in voting for the amendment. But 203 MPs followed the Government's position by voting no and the day was lost.[153]

## Chapter Seven

Ahead of the 1997 General Election, Mr Mackinlay was
confident his campaign would be successful. The Tories
had become hugely unpopular with little chance of
electoral success, and support for the pardons across
Labour appeared to be broad. 'There was tacit, implicit,
overwhelming endorsement of me, that's why I was even
more staggered by John Reid when we came into
government,' he said.

'In terms of my ego, people were congratulating me,
people were coming to me and saying well done, people
wanted to talk about it because it is a thing which is so
interesting.' Mr Mackinlay said: 'Certainly I think I would
have got tacit support from John Smith. The rule was that
shadow ministers don't normally sign Early Day Motions
but there were nods and winks, everybody approved of
this. It was popular.'

National media coverage of the case for pardons was
increasing and with Harry Farr, there was an image that
allowed them to focus on the human impact of the strict
military discipline of the First World War.

Mr Mackinlay said: 'You've got a grave injustice case
well documented, you've got wife alive, you've got
daughter alive and you've got a photo of him. And he
looks great. What a proud decent man. The photograph is
iconic and has been reproduced around the world. It
wouldn't have been the same story without it. The picture
is superb. I think it was so important, that picture.'

When Tony Blair came to power in 1997, Mr Mackinlay
was confident of his support after his 1995 comments that
he supported a review of all of the cases. Yet the new
Prime Minister's view on the matter was not publically
advanced, and his support was not signalled again for
almost another decade.

Labour's election victory should have been the culmination of Mr Mackinlay's campaign, but the chance was soon lost. He said: 'When governments come in they have some high-profile gesture things to show they were up and running and I assumed it would be in that category because it didn't cost any money, it was popular and I just thought it would happen.'

Dr John Reid, who had voted for a pardon just two years earlier as a shadow minister, was made Minister of State for the Armed Forces and in May 1997 he announced a review to consider the case for pardoning the 306 executed soldiers. As part of the review, Dr Reid and senior civil servants spoke to Mr Putkowski and Judge Babington, the two authors who were considered authorities on the executions.

Those present included the Judge Advocate, James Rant; an MoD historian; a press officer and a civil service adviser, who Mr Putkowski believes was a Navy commodore. Mr Putkowski said: 'I think there could have been more than half a dozen, sitting on a settee, me on a chair in front of them.

'The issue that came out fairly quickly was Reid had been given a third of the files and he actually sat down and read them. But they had been cherry-picked. He said "I have looked at it and I can't see any reason for a pardon". He said it was very hard. I said "fine, I have looked at all of the files and I give you another 100 that would call that into question".

'I didn't want to argue, I wasn't in that position. As far as I knew the report wasn't written, the fact I now know the report had been written and we were brought in as an after-thought, really as decoration so they could say there had been consultation which was bollocks from one end to the other. Reid himself was steered very much by his civil servants, they just said "there isn't a case, there is nothing we can do about it".

'Murmurings of "wasn't it a terrible business. Names on the war memorials which was complete nonsense because the war memorials were run by various agencies and local authorities and so on. It wasn't in the gift of the Government to tell who was going to go on the war memorials and who wasn't. Reid said "look I haven't been contacted by any of the families". I said "look I've contacted them all".

'I had 30 or 40 letters, from each of the families and I said actually I have minister, here. I wish I could have bottled the expressions that were on the faces round there because I think it must have been very evident to Reid that actually nobody had been trying too hard. At the time I asked all the families to write and I said I'll just give them to the minister. I think what I wanted to do at that point, I knew there would be a dossier on this somewhere and I wanted the families' point of view to be there. This was me as a historian, I knew evidence would not be destroyed so it would be tucked inside and I wanted it there. I didn't have great hopes but I thought it would go.'

Hopes were high among other campaigners but in March 1998 the Daily Mail ran a front-page exclusive with the headline: 'No pardon for shot soldiers'. Political reporter Andrew Sparrow described the decision not to pardon the soldiers as a 'Labour U-turn'. He wrote: 'According to Government insiders, the review has confirmed that proper military and judicial procedures were carried out before the men were executed. Although the outcome might seem harsh by modern standards, official rules were not broken.'[154]

In July that year, Dr Reid stood before the Commons to explain why the Government would not be instigating the legislation that would lead to the resolution so many people wanted to see. He said the Government had considered every aspect of the cases including the legal basis for the trials – the field general courts martial. Its conclusion was the procedures followed were correct, 'given the law as it stood at the time'[155].

Considering medical records, he said that most did not make 'implicit or explicit reference to nervous, or other psychological or medical, disorders'.[156] He added: 'However frustrating, the passage of time means that the grounds for a blanket legal pardon on the basis of unsafe conviction does not exist.'

Looking instead at the cases individually, Mr Reid pointed to three possibilities for a legal pardon – a full pardon, a conditional pardon or a statutory pardon. The free pardon would remove the convictions of the soldiers and, as a consequence, the subsequent death penalty. The conditional pardon would mean the conviction would remain, but the sentence would be removed from the man's record. Finally, the statutory pardon would require an act of parliament to ensure its validity.

However, he added that all required concrete evidence for overturning the decision of a court and went on to explain that, having examined 100 of the cases personally, there was little to be found to aid such as move. He said: 'I have accepted legal advice that, in the vast majority of cases, there is little to be gleaned from the fragments of the stories that would provide serious grounds for a legal pardon.'

His argument was that due to insufficient evidence, if the Government was to proceed on a case-by-case basis there was likelihood that many of the soldiers would be likely to be re-condemned, whether they were guilty or not.

To Mr Mackinlay, it was like a 'dagger through the heart'. Given just a few hours' notice before Dr Reid stood up to announce the decision, an emotional Mr Mackinlay had to decide how to react, whether to express his anger and frustration or to remain dignified out of respect for his supporters and the descendants of Harry Farr and others. He had spent many hundreds of hours on the subject, and so had key supporters.

He chose the latter course, but he believes it meant that some people thought he had sold out given that Labour were in power and had not pushed forward, something he was deeply affected by.

He said: 'I thought this is what a Labour government should be doing. It was a class issue. It was non-commissioned, the ordinary oik who were executed. It was not the upper-crust, there was a clear divide and after all so many of these men who were executed were physically frail, many of them were youngsters, they weren't articulate, they couldn't defend themselves. There was stress. It was absolutely an issue of rights.'

Mr Mackinlay felt Dr Reid had been leant upon by civil servants, who were institutionally against the idea of admitting wrongdoing, however ancient. The defeat was a bitter blow, made harder to take by the fact that time was marching on, veterans of the Great War were dwindling in number and, as a consequence, the issue was becoming more historic and less relevant to living British citizens.

It was a blow for the Shot At Dawn campaigners as well. Mr Putkowski said: 'The Labour Party had come to power, we had rather hoped a pardon had gone through, it wasn't, it was knocked on the head, I rather suspect partly it was because the Government at the time having just come to power, Tony Blair having just being elected to power, they were trying to put through the Strategic Defence Review (SDR). The SDR was for the post-Communist era defence of this country.

'That required a core group of about 24 senior civil servants at the MoD to work with the Labour Party, the incoming minister and Government, to formulate what was to be the future of the defence of this country. The last thing they wanted was to rub up the MoD and the MoD really didn't like the SAD campaign. They really, really didn't like it. It wasn't just asking for a change of policy which would have been extra work, it was visceral.'

However, there were some positives taken by some campaigners from Dr Reid's decision. During his speech he had said that he recognised that the executed soldiers were victims of war and added: 'We hope other outside the House will recognise all that, and that they will consider allowing the missing names to be added to books of remembrance and war memorials throughout the land.'[157] What made Dr Reid, who achieved a BA in history at the Open University as well as a PhD in the subject, change his position from broad support to refusal is unclear. He refused a request for an interview for this book.

But he did offer a number of conciliatory gestures to campaigners, saying the House expressed a deep sense of regret at the loss of life. He stopped short of an apology, however. Finally, he promised that the Defence Secretary would consider the abolition of the death penalty for military offences including serious misconduct in action, assisting the enemy and mutiny.

These capital crimes were abolished later in the year with the Human Rights Act 1998 being passed, but this merely pre-empted the signing of a Council of Europe treaty. In 2002 Britain signed protocol 13 of Treaty 187, which ensured the death penalty was abandoned by Britain for all offences.[158]

In response to the statement, Mr Mackinlay re-stated his belief that a formal pardon was still possible and his hope to attempt legislation in the future. However, his tone throughout was conciliatory, and he thanked Dr Reid, saying: 'Parliament has now reflected the fact that they should be acknowledged as the victims of the Great War along with the many other millions.'

Mike Hancock, the Liberal Democrat MP for Portsmouth South, said he believed 'countless millions of people will not understand why it is impossible for the House to grant a pardon.' He said that pardoning truly guilty men as a result of a group pardon was a price the nation was willing to pay.

However, Keith Simpson, Conservative MP for mid-Norfolk and the Tories' spokesman on the issue, who previously opposed the pardoning of the soldiers said he did not believe Dr Reid should have made a statement of regret. He said: 'Last year the Prime Minister expressed regret over the Irish potato famine, an action which many people agreed with. However, we have to consider, where does this begin and end?'[159]

Dr Reid spoke again, to dismiss rumours of a cover-up and to insist that his expression of regret was not re-writing history, it was actually a way of interpreting it. The decision was met with a mixed reaction. The Western Front Association described it as 'fair and acceptable', but while the Royal British Legion welcomed the 'deep sense of regret' expressed by Dr Reid, it said the lack of pardons was disappointing.[160]

Reaction among relatives who had thrown their weight behind the Shot At Dawn campaign was stronger. Tom Stones, whose great-uncle Joseph Stones was executed in 1917, said Dr Reid's decision was a 'fudge'. He told the Guardian: 'This is not the Government speaking, it's the Army. It knows it did a shameful thing and is closing ranks.'[161]

Judge Babington wrote to The Times to protest the decision. He revealed that he had been invited by Dr Reid to the Ministry of Defence to give his thoughts on the cases and had told the minister that he believed a number of the convictions were 'so unsatisfactory that they should be immediately reversed'.

He said: 'I mentioned the three 17-year-old youths who were shot for desertion, the men who previously had been wounded in action or had been treated for what was then called shell-shock, and the soldiers whose nerves had cracked in the fearful conditions of the Western Front. Dr Reid said that one of his difficulties had been that many of the files were incomplete, which made it virtually impossible in some cases to tell if an injustice had been done.

'He felt that if only certain men were pardoned it might be inferred that the remainder had been properly convicted and sentenced. This seems to me to be an inadequate reason for refusing pardons where the files show that an injustice has occurred.'[162]

Prior to the decision, campaigners felt that public support continued to be with them, which was demonstrated when relatives of the executed men were invited to a war memorial event for the first time. In May 1998, Janet and Jim Booth were invited to attend a service of remembrance to mark 80 years since the end of the First World War in Croydon, south London. The event was attended by 20 veterans of the conflict with an age range between 97 and 106 years.

One of the elderly veterans said to Janet: 'It could have been any one of us here (alluding to being executed).' It was the first time that a member of Harry's family had been invited to such an event and showed that veterans of the conflict made no distinctions when commemorating the First World War dead. It was also a very visible show of support for the campaign for the 306 soldiers to be pardoned.

In September 1998, in a bid to make a fresh push for pardons Janet and Mr Putkowski were joined by film critic Barry Norman and former Labour leader Michael Foot in launching a postcard campaign. Mr Foot and Mr Norman signed the first postcards to be sent to the Armed Forces Minister, Doug Henderson, and Prime Minister Tony Blair.

They were photographed at the Roundhouse in Camden, north London where cast members of the National Youth Theatre's production of *Oh! What A Lovely War* supported the publicity drive.[163] The following month the actors and actresses sent an open letter to Mr Henderson, which was published in The Observer. They said: 'We ask you refer the cases to an independent judicial enquiry and that you act on the judges' recommendations. Where miscarriages of justice occurred, pardons should be issued. We will not let these men be forgotten. We will not let history seal their fate in silence.'[164]

Later in 1998, on the day before Remembrance Sunday, relatives including Janet and Gertie were permitted to lay wreaths at the Cenotaph for the first time, albeit at a separate ceremony. The Royal British Legion's hierarchy would not allow the families of soldiers who had been executed in the First World War to march alongside veterans during the main Remembrance Sunday parade. The alternative event was organised by Tom Stones who was another important Shot At Dawn campaigner during the 1990s. His uncle Joseph William Stones was executed for 'shamefully casting away arms'.

Mr Stones first learned of his uncle's fate when he researched his family history and discovered that Willy's name had been scored out of the family bible, something that demonstrates the shame and revulsion felt about those who were stigmatised as cowards.[165]

Mr Stones was an academic and a leading expert on potatoes. He was also an accomplished public speaker, an expert researcher and someone who threw their weight fully behind the campaign. Mr Putkowski, who worked with him on the campaign, said: 'Tom Stones in the 1990s really was very important. He was kind of very clued up on how to do things. Tom was the biz and also he did his homework. He knew everything.

'He went round talking to schools, he turned up and insisted on Willy Stones being put on the war memorial in Crook in County Durham. It was he who organised the gatherings in Whitehall. Tom went out and organised, he said right you have Armistice Day, we will have our Armistice Day.'

Gertie Harris and Janet were also at the parade – to pay their respects but also to appear as a visible reminder to the Government that they were not prepared to go away, to accept the lack of pardons. With them was Janet's husband Jim, Harry's granddaughter Valerie Jackson, his great-granddaughter Karen Jackson and several of Gertie's cousins – John Farr and his daughter and Bert Farr and his sons.

Mr Putkowski said: 'So they turned up there and I think Gertie was in a wheelchair by then because she was all wrapped up, and that was the only occasion, the nearest thing to a national rally that we had. What it was was two or three dozen people, all the rest were journalists, we were outnumbered by them, and we all did stuff to camera afterwards, always.'

Gertie told the BBC: 'It's such an honour to feel that we can now recognise our soldiers that were wrongly executed in the First World War.'[166] Indeed, Janet remembers her mother as a great ambassador for the Shot At Dawn campaign and a natural in front of the TV cameras. She spoke eloquently about how she learned of her father's fate aged in her mid-40s, the shock and upset she suffered and how her family had suffered shame and stigma.

Although not part of the main event the following day, 200 people had gathered to lay crosses, wreaths and poppies at the country's central memorial. At 11am, a lone bugler played The Last Post, which was followed by a minute's silence. Mr Mackinlay, seemingly undeterred by Dr Reid's statement earlier in the year, was determined to increase pressure for pardons on the Government.

At the event, he said: 'This commemoration is the launch of a renewed campaign I believe is supported by the majority of MPs.[167] I think the public interest in this event shows that gaining pardons for soldiers killed in this way is a massive issue. The Government needs to look at it closely.'[168] Although it was a poignant occasion, its solemnity was diminished by the fact that the roads were not properly closed and the silence of Remembrance Sunday was not achieved.

The following year the Press were beginning to look at the event a little more critically in terms of how the establishment was not embracing the families and campaigners. On November 13 1999, families again gathered by The Cenotaph on the Saturday before Remembrance Sunday.

Writing in the Observer, John Sweeney said: 'Eight decades on from the end of the First World War, the 306 British soldiers shot for desertion are still dishonoured, still shamed, still the subject of the official disapproval of Her Majesty's Government. The microphone at the Cenotaph had been turned off, and the traffic kept at bay for only a brief moment by the police. The homage of Labour MP Andrew Mackinlay – "We shall remember them" - was all but sabotaged as a silver Saab revved up and the exhaust of a souped-up superbike echoed across Whitehall.'

The message was clear – the lack of official recognition of these men as victims of war without distinction from those who were killed in the traditional sense was as shabby as the unofficial ceremony at The Cenotaph.

Britain was not the only country where activists were seeking to challenge the status quo concerning the executions. In New Zealand, the campaign for pardons was focused on five men who were members of the New Zealand Expeditionary Force and were executed in the First World War.

Mark Peck, a Labour MP for Invercargill, first became aware of the apparent injustice behind the executions when he was contacted by a constituent in 1995. A constituent and friend of his approached him for help in finding information about one of the men, whose case remained classified.

Like Judge Babington in Britain, military historian Christopher Pugsley had been given access to the official records for his 1991 book On the Fringe of Hell, which was about New Zealand soldiers and military discipline in the First World War. Citing this access as a precedent, Mr Peck was granted access to the files, despite the fact a 100-year exclusion remained. Four of the men were deserters and one was executed for mutiny over a prison riot. All were volunteers.

Private John Braithwaite, of Second Battalion, Otago Regiment, was charged with committing mutiny during an incident on August 28 1916, tried and found guilty of the offence on October 11 and executed 18 days later.[169]

Private Frank Hughes, of Second Battalion, Canterbury Regiment, was charged with committing desertion on July 29 1916. He was tried and found guilty on August 12 and executed 13 days later.

Private John King, of the same regiment's First Battalion, was charged with committing desertion on May 30 1917. He was tried and found guilty on August 5 and executed exactly two weeks after. Private Victor Manson Spencer, of First Battalion, Otago Regiment, was charged with committing desertion on August 13 1917.

He was tried and found guilty on January 17 the following year. Twelve days later he was again sentenced to death after the date of his desertion was revised. He was finally executed on February 24, 1918. Private John Joseph Sweeney, of the First Battalion, Otago Regiment, was charged with committing the offence of desertion on July 25 1916. He was tried and found guilty on September 13 and executed on October 2.

Mr Peck resolved to campaign to pardon the five, believing their deaths should never have occurred. He said: 'The thing that crystallised it for me very early on was Spencer's file. When I opened the file, there was a piece of military report paper and scrawled across it in black pencil was the word DEATH and it was the most chilling thing I ever read. The rest of the file paled into insignificance really except for Spencer's own handwritten plea to the court for leniency on the basis that he had been recently bombarded and he was suffering from the effects of drink. That fell on deaf ears. That handwritten note was quite emotional (for me), frankly.'

After speaking with the clerk of the New Zealand Parliament in Wellington about how to proceed, the politician decided to attempt a Private Member's Bill. For it to be considered, the bill had to be correctly drafted, show a clear issue and also a remedy. When it complied with the parliament's requirements, it was entered into a ballot along with other such bills and Mr Peck was forced to wait.

In 1996, new national elections were held and upon re-election, Mr Peck ensured the bill remained live so that it could be drawn from the ballot, which it was just before the 1999 elections. The bill was carried by 112 votes to eight at its first reading and at the select committee stage it was suggested that a report be commissioned to look at the five cases and assess whether they were deemed worthy of pardons.

Edward Summers, a former judge, was asked to make recommendations about how to proceed. His report stated that although he believed injustices had occurred and concluded that all five men had suffered some form of shell-shock, which could have played a part in the offences for which they were executed for[170], it was not suitable to judge the behaviour of the time by those in authority by modern standards.

Instead of pardons, he recommended that the Government instead apologise to the families of the men, something which Mr Peck disagreed with, so he made the issue of the pardons central to his re-election campaign. Mr Peck said he encountered little opposition to his bill but the leadership of the Royal New Zealand Returned and Services' Association, the country's equivalent of the Royal British Legion, did raise concerns about the move. National President David Cox, speaking in June 2000, claimed the association's official position was not opposed to pardons for all 306 men, but that it felt it was inequitable to pardon the five. He said: 'You can't forget about the rest. If you're going to do it for one, then you must do it for all.'[171] But the comments sparked outrage among rank and file members.

Mr Peck said: 'They had a mutiny on their hands because NSA branches around the country got hold of the national office and let them have it. The old buggers around the country were saying what happened to these soldiers was an absolute injustice.'

Labour gained power that year and the bill was adopted by the new Government, led by Helen Clark. It gave the proposal impetus and guaranteed a final majority, but had to be vetted by sub-committee before it could finally be voted in. The biggest change to its original drafting was to write in a clause ensuring that no compensation was to be paid to families, similar to the stance of campaigners in Britain.

This was to be a symbolic victory - recognition of wrongdoing rather than any kind of personal gain for the families involved. During the passage of the bill, Mr Peck met ancestors of the five men - many of whom were present in parliament for its third reading. He said: 'The fascinating thing was with the Spencer family, the family remained involved in the military. Two of the family served in Vietnam and were taken aside by the family before they went and were advised there was a stain of dishonour and they weren't to add to that particular stain of dishonour.

'They always wondered what it was about. The old guy would never talk about it so when I did the bill I went down to meet them. Very strong old men, they were in tears when I first met them and it was almost always the same with every other family I met. They were so grateful that this thing was being dealt with and that they could take the skeleton out of the closet and not have to worry about the stain of dishonour. You have no idea about the shame people felt as a result of those executions.'

Mr Peck also spoke to the granddaughter of a soldier who was ordered to carry out the executions as part of the firing squad in the case of Spencer, who was apparently from the same battalion. 'He just never got over it and was a broken man,' she told Mr Peck. Similarly, relatives of the chaplain who was present also explained how he was troubled by it for the rest of his life.

Another military judge assessed the case of Braithwaite and concluded that such was the injustice, campaigners should pursue a quashing of his original conviction as well as the official pardon, but this was not something that was achieved. Mr Peck said: 'We never managed to get to that point but it made me think we were on very strong ground in respect of issues that were in the bill.'

In September 2000, the Great War Act[172] was passed to pardon the five, removing their convictions. Its stated intention was 'to remove, so far as practicable, the dishonour that the execution of those five soldiers brought to those soldiers and their families'.

Its effect would be 'to recognise that the execution of the five soldiers to whom those pardons are granted was not a fate that they deserved but was one that resulted from - (a) the harsh discipline that was believed at the time to be required; and (b) the application of the death penalty for military offences being seen at that time as an essential part of maintaining military discipline'.

In particular, the records of the five men were to be updated to include the pardon and the Commonwealth War Graves Commission was to be informed of the action. The act was granted Royal Assent on September 14 2000. It was front-page news in New Zealand, and made headlines in Britain too. The fact that the Queen was effectively granting pardons to the five men was heartening for campaigners in Britain and to Mr Peck.

Mr Peck was contacted by members of the Shot At Dawn campaign who were keen to draw on his experiences to help push for pardons in Britain. He also spoke to Canadian authorities, because a similar bill was also being prepared there, though the closest they got to a pardon in that country was the names of 22 soldiers added to a book of remembrance in the country's parliament in December 2001.[173]

Mr Peck said: 'This issue found me, I didn't go looking for it. Once I found it I was very consumed by it because the injustice that had occurred was pretty clear and the guys couldn't speak for themselves and their families certainly hadn't spoken for themselves so I was determined we needed to get something done about it. I was absolutely blown away by how far through New Zealand society the effect of those executions had gone.'

## Chapter Eight

In late 2000, relatives of some of the 306 executed men were told they could join the Remembrance Sunday service at The Cenotaph for the first time. The decision to allow the group to march in the parade felt extremely significant to campaigners, adding a sense of legitimacy to their cause. The British Legion had announced its support for the campaign the previous year and the presence of relatives was part of a wider decision to allow civilians to join the parade for the first time.

It was a crisp autumnal morning when Janet and her husband Jim pushed Gertie along Whitehall in her wheelchair with her legs covered in a blanket to protect her from the chill air. The Shot At Dawn campaigners took their places alongside hundreds of other civilians who were representing organisations such as Second World War evacuees, the Auxiliary Fire Service, the Women's Land Army and even the Scouts.

Also present were the familiar faces of the War Widows Association, members of which had joined the Shot At Dawn campaigners the previous year at their Saturday Cenotaph service. Valerie, Janet's sister and Harry's granddaughter also joined the parade with her husband Fred, a veteran himself who wore his father's and his own medals on his chest.

Janet said: 'As I looked around the group I saw the many faces of the Shot At Dawn campaigners. The loyal supporters who gave their time freely for the cause. Andy DeComyn, a sculptor who was working on a statue of an executed soldier for the National Memorial Arboretum was there that day together with his wife and their little girl. The child stood quietly standing next to her parents in a colourful coat adorned with her great grandfather's medals. A pretty hat, gloves and boots completed her outfit but she looked very tiny standing there among the adults.

'Andy had started going amongst the supporters with a small pot of white paint. He was dipping the paintbrush into the paint and covering the black centre of the red poppy white. The white centre was to represent the piece of material which was placed over the condemned soldier's heart so the firing squad could aim at their target.'

Other relatives included Tom Stones who represented his uncle Sergeant William Stones, Nora High who was there for her uncle Private William Nelson and Terry Morrish, now wheelchair-bound, to remember his uncle Driver James Swaine. The family of Jamaican Private Herbert Morris of the British West Indies Regiment, who was executed aged just 17, were also there.

In one of the most shocking cases among the 306, Private Morris was not medically examined for his trial despite complaining of a nervous condition and had no prisoner's friend at the Court Martial.[174]

He was found guilty of desertion and shot by firing squad in Belgium on September 20 1917.

Support for the boy soldier who was buried thousands of miles from home in Poperinghe New Military Cemetery also came from Jamaican policemen who were resplendent in their smart uniforms.

Silence fell as the service began after the marchers formed up in their groups along Whitehall. The group of about 50 relatives and campaigners stood under the banner of the World War One Pardons Campaign.

This permitted name was a toned-down version of what the group had better become known as – Shot At Dawn or SAD – but inclusion in the Remembrance Day Parade was much more important to such concerns for those present on this special day. However, one member of the campaign carried a stark cross engraved with '306' and 'SHOT AT DAWN'.

Situated near the rear of the formation, the group watched the service on the large screens put up along the road for the benefit of those taking part and the crowds of people in attendance, up to 10 deep on the pavements. Janet said: 'As if by some divine intervention, just as Big Ben struck 11am, the clouds parted and a shaft of sunlight shone down upon the Cenotaph. A cannon fired in the distance to mark the start of the two minutes' silence, followed by the bugles sounding the Last Post.'

The Queen laid her wreath of poppies at the base of the Cenotaph, followed by Prince Phillip and the other members of the Royal family. Prime Minister Tony Blair and the Leader of the Opposition, William Hague, laid their tributes.

Janet said: 'I looked around me at the different Regiments, their groups now quite depleted over the years but it made me proud to be British. Many of the men now in wheelchairs, pushed by their comrades, who themselves were having difficulty in walking, either from wounds inflicted during combat or just old age.'

The old soldiers, sailors and airmen marched off to the tunes of *Pack Up Your Troubles in Your Old Kit Bag* and *It's a Long Way to Tipperary* played by the Massed Bands of the Guards Division and the pipes and drums of First Battalion, Royal Scots.

Janet said: 'Eventually, it is our turn to march. The gentleman from the British Legion at the side of us shouting orders – "left, right, left right, keep up, keep in step". As we passed the Cenotaph, he shouts – "eyes left", then "eyes front".

'We march on, the crowds clapping as we pass them. We make a right turn back on to Horse Guards Parade and are given an order for "eyes right" as we pass Princess Anne who was on the podium taking the salute.

'How her arm must have ached that day. It made me think of how the mothers, wives, girlfriends and loved ones must have felt when their men didn't come back from the wars. How their hearts must have ached at the loss of the men in their lives. How my own grandmother must have felt when my grandfather never returned from France at the end of the First World War. She always watched the old veterans on TV marching proudly past the Cenotaph on Remembrance Day. As she watched in later life she would say. "my Harry should have been there marching with the soldiers".'

Gertie was the focus of a Daily Mail article by Richard Kay, which recognised the historic moment in which family members were allowed to lay wreaths in front of the Queen. He wrote: 'Eighty-four years after her father was shot for cowardice, Mrs Harris was at last allowed to honour his memory clutching an old family snapshot and a red poppy as she was pushed down Whitehall in a wheelchair.

'Their presence brought respectful applause from spectators – 10 deep on the pavements saluting them every bit as much as the bemedalled veterans in whose footsteps they followed.' Janet told the paper: 'We have righted a wrong. All those shot were war heroes anyway, brave enough to have volunteered in the first place.'[175]

In the Daily Mirror, Gertie was pictured holding a photograph of Harry at the Cenotaph. She said: 'This is the proudest day of my life. My father joined the Army when he was 18 because he believed in defending his country. After the war broke out he fought bravely for five months in the trenches before being sent to hospital with shell-shock. His mind and body were so shattered he couldn't even hold a pen to write to my mother. The only letter she received was written by a nurse, who explained he was trembling too much to write.'[176]

Step by step the campaign was gaining legitimacy. From a lack of official recognition to being a full part of Britain's annual act of remembrance and seeing some of the 306 men pardoned in New Zealand, there was a feeling of real progress at this time. However, Defence Secretary Geoff Hoon had that week attempted to dampen down the renewed clamour for pardons. Appearing on GMTV, he said that it would 'not be appropriate' to issue them.

---

When Dr Reid spoke in the House of Commons to announce that the executed men would not be pardoned in 1998, he attempted to strike a note of conciliation by urging 'all organisations' – taken to mean parish councils, charities and regimental associations – to recognise the executed men as victims of war. It was something of an empty gesture from a man who had the power to legally recognise their status as victims, but it was a small degree of progress nonetheless.

Many organisations already recognised the men as soldiers to be honoured and mourned, not criminals as they continued to be viewed in the eyes of the government and the military. For example, the Durham Light Infantry already listed the names of the executed men in its book of remembrance.

And from the very beginning, the War Graves Commission had not discriminated against the executed soldiers whose bodies were not lost. They were laid to rest in the same cemetery as their fallen comrades, not hidden away in separate areas.

The vast majority of the inscriptions on the grave stones do not say that the dead men were executed either, in a small gesture which could be viewed as one of shame by those in power, or one of humanity, depending on your view point. Parish councillors and local newspapers, still following the campaign with vigour in many areas of Britain, were embracing the spirit of reconciliation off their own backs.

Some councils decided to pass a motion to add a name of a long-lost local boy who was previously excluded. In Newcastle-Upon-Tyne in July 1999, a special service of remembrance and reconciliation was held at St Silas Church for Private Peter Giles. Private Giles, a Northumberland Fusilier from that parish, was executed on August 24 1916. Members of the British Legion attended in large numbers, with 30 standard bearers at the church.[177] The presence of members of the Legion showed how far the campaign for pardons had come. The organisation had previously been against exonerating the 306 executed men but at its annual conference in 1999 a motion was carried 'with just one dissenting voice'. A report in the British Legion magazine said: 'The Government says too many files have been lost or destroyed for individual cases to be re-examined at this late stage. The Legion believes a general amnesty or exoneration to mark the new millennium would remove the burden of shame, guilt and resentment from the families of those executed.'[178] However, the move to add names to war memorials also sparked controversy. In Shoreham, Kent, a motion was put before the parish council to add the name of Private Thomas Highgate, the first soldier to be executed by the British Army in the First World War. Private Highgate fought during the retreat from Mons and was charged with desertion in September 1914. He was found guilty and executed just two days later, after being given less than an hour's notice that he was to be shot by firing squad after his death sentence had been confirmed by the commander-in-chief. He died aged 19.

After what was described as an 'agonising meeting' of the council in February 2000, seven members decided against adding Private Highgate's name to the monument in his home village.[179] The decision sparked uproar and led to the parish priest conducting a referendum of villagers on the matter, with the majority of those who voted in favour of adding the name – 170 voted for and 46 voted against.[180] Yet the councillors stood firm and in extraordinary scenes at a subsequent meeting, vicar Barry Simmonds was jeered as he pleaded for compassion and one villager broke down in tears.

After the May meeting, when council voted 5-2 against including the name, Jean Lothian, the chairman, said: 'In 1920 when the memorial was built, it was the villagers of Shoreham who decided whose names should be added. We can't rewrite history in this way.'[181] Campaigner John Hipkin said of the decision: 'The council is out of step with many councils throughout the UK who have, since 1919, honoured the victims of British firings squads in World War One.'[182]

The campaign was beginning to draw international attention and in March 2000 Janet was invited to attend a conference in Belgium with her mother. Piet Chielens, director of the In Flanders Fields Museum, was hosting the event in May, called Unquiet Graves.

Although Janet and Gertie were unable to attend, Julian Putkowski was a key speaker, telling the story of the campaign. Mr Putksowski said: 'He (Mr Chielens) said the museum is a peace museum and it needed to open up a narrative about unquiet graves. In other words, graves which raised question marks or where issues were unsettled, about the unfinished small business of war.

'The conference itself was important, not because it happened in Ypres or that it was particularly well covered here, it was because it went out on the World Service so 170m people got to hear about it. It also drew the Government's attention to the fact that there were going to be policy issues about it.'

Also in March, Mr Mackinlay launched his latest attempt to pass a bill on the matter. Identical in its content, it was ordered to be read a second time the following month, yet once again it was timed out.

That year, Mr DeComyn completed work on a memorial to commemorate the 306 British and Empire soldiers executed for military offences in the First World War. The memorial was to be sited at the National Memorial Arboretum in Alrewas near Lichfield, Staffordshire, which was opened in May 2001 as a place of tribute to servicemen and women killed in war.

Mr DeComyn's memorial - a gift from the artist to the surviving relatives of the executed men – was striking in its simplicity. Featuring a young soldier, tied to a stake with hands behind his back, the most prominent feature was a blindfold covering the subject's eyes. In front of him stand six fir trees to represent a firing squad.

This stark representation of the vulnerability of those executed in their final moments was heightened by Mr DeComyn's inspiration for the 10ft-tall statue – 17-year-old Private Herbert Burden. Private Burden was one of the youngest soldiers to be executed by the British Army – if not the youngest. He joined the Northumberland Fusiliers by lying about his age and went to France in March 1915.[183] By July he was standing trial for desertion, was found guilty and executed on July 21. He has no known grave and is commemorated at the Menin Gate memorial. Surrounding the new statue were hundreds of stakes to represent all of the 306 men who died, complete with their names.

In 1999 the artist was in his final year of an art and design degree as a mature student at the University of Central England, now Birmingham City University. Ready to take on a major public project, Mr DeComyn quickly found it was impossible to receive a commission without previously being commissioned. To counter this chicken-and-egg scenario, he decided to take on a project at his own expense to start off his portfolio.

The sculpture was to be made in a durable cement-based material making it strong but cheaper than stone or bronze and all that Mr DeComyn needed was a compelling subject to begin work on. On Remembrance Sunday 1999 he watched a documentary about the work of Mr Hipkin on the Shot At Dawn campaign and said that he instantly knew how he was going to proceed.

He said: 'I was going to build a memorial dedicated to the 306 and especially for those who were too young to fight. I started work on a design and quickly fixed on the image of a young, blindfolded soldier with his hands tied behind his back. It was important to me to portray youth and vulnerability and was thus representative of underage boy soldiers, two of which were known at the time.'

Mr DeComyn contacted Mr Hipkin to consult him on his and relatives' views on his project and received a prompt and positive response. As he worked on the project, he began to approach the subject of where to site it. The Royal British Legion did not have a suitable location but put Mr DeComyn in touch with David Childs who was in the process of setting up the National Memorial Arboretum.

Mr Childs threw his weight behind the project and suggested they plant 306 trees to commemorate the soldier but this was to prove impractical. Instead he suggested that 306 posts were set up in a 'Greek Theatre' which was to symbolise the tragedy of their deaths. Mr DeComyn initiated an 'adopt a soldier' campaign and quickly covered the cost of installing the posts.

On June 21 2001, just a month after the official opening of the National Arboretum, the Shot At Dawn memorial was unveiled. The ceremony was attended by relatives and campaigners, prominent among whom were Gertie, Janet and Mr Hipkin. Gertie was given the honour of unveiling the statue and said: 'I am very proud and very grateful that now we have somewhere we can come and pay honour to those soldiers who I consider were wrongly executed. Most were suffering from post-traumatic stress, which today is recognised as an illness.'

Mr Childs had recommended to Mr DeComyn that she officially reveal his work of art and although the pair had never met before, he later said he found her captivating. He said: 'It was an enormously proud day for me and I never expected that it would capture so much imagination or publicity. For me it was just a way of commemorating a group of soldiers where they couldn't be influenced by local councils and nay-sayers. It was a place where families and supporters could finally pay their respects in a dignified way and where government had no influence.'

Recalling the ceremony, Janet said: 'We were not involved with any of the arrangements – that was down to Andy. We just had to turn up on the day and mum unveiled the statue which was a great honour for her and Harry Farr's family.' The family were not aware of any criticism of the decision to open the memorial at the time and Mr DeComyn said that unlike the opposition to the pardons themselves there were few dissenting voices when his work was unveiled.

He said: 'It would seem that people accepted the commemoration even if they didn't agree with pardons. I always felt that commemoration was the very least that they deserved as they were simply victims of war and none of them would have died in that manner had war not taken place. When asked why I made the memorial my response is "because I could" and, like the pardons, is a matter of giving people the benefit of the doubt. I count myself fortunate that I have never been put in such a situation as those men and boys, and could not possibly judge them in any way.'

In 2001 Cathryn Corns and John Hughes-Wilson published the most exhaustive study yet of the First World War military executions. Meticulously researched, the book examined the various category of military discipline offences, the killings of under-age soldiers and the statistical context of the executions. Its tone and conclusions fall very much in line with anti-pardons arguments – that some of those condemned to die – not all – were very much guilty of the offences of which they were convicted.

Consequently, they were subject to the punishments of the time, however harsh they may appear in the present-day. Indeed, the authors gave short shrift to some elements of the Shot At Dawn campaign, saying it concentrated on a 'broad-brush approach of what Americans call "shroud-waving" and a shared sense of injustice'.

They said: 'The truth is that the Pardons Campaign by the turn of the century had become a highly vocal protest group, a loose alliance about the alleged grievances of a small group of men legally executed more than 80 years ago. It had become a matter of radical and regional politics driven principally by emotion and a sense of grievance or some hope of financial compensation, rather than hard fact.'[184]

The authors may well have had valid points in their opinion of the campaign, but in one area they were patently wrong.  Not once had any relative of the executed men demanded compensation for their family's loss. This statement by the authors was a serious misjudgment of the motives of those involved.

In May of that year, Mr Mackinlay presented his latest bill to Parliament, another doomed to fail but another pertinent reminder to the Government that the campaign was still in full voice. And though few major in-roads were made in the following few years, campaigners refused to be silenced.

In Ireland, an independent yet related movement had grown up, with supporters lobbying the Irish government for a pardon for 26 Irishman who were executed for military offences and made up part of the overall 306 victims of the firing squad. A former merchant seaman, Peter Mulvany, had driven the campaign, crucially gaining support from both sides of the Catholic-Protestant divide.

In truth, this was easily achieved because of the devastation suffered by communities in the north and south in terms of the thousands upon thousands of lives lost during the conflict. As early as autumn 1914, three Irish divisions were in France amid a patriotic recruitment surge by those wanting to protect Great Britain and an independent Ireland. They were the 36th, or the Ulster Division, and the Irish divisions, the 10th and the 16th.[185] Their losses, including at such iconic battles including at the Somme, would be heart-breakingly prodigious.

Mr Mulvany spent a number of years on his project and in 2003 he made a major breakthrough – Ireland's then Minister for Foreign Affairs Brian Cowen agreed to take the matter up with British government officials. And so seriously was the matter being taken that a 'damning' report was prepared by the Irish Government to back its claims.

Mr Mulvany said: 'All I expected was a letter coming from the Irish Government simply expressing support. When I was told the officials were writing a report I nearly fell off the chair. I did not expect that.'[186] The report was completed in October 2004 and sent to the Ministry of Defence in London. Despite meetings and further requests from the Irish side, no formal response had been made by the British Government by the end of the following year.[187] The Irish pressure was welcomed by British campaigners, with Janet having written to the MoD enclosing a new petition she had signed advocating pardons for Irish soldiers. In response, civil servant Alexandra Ward revealed that 'a meeting has already been held at official level to examine the issues. Further contact is expected'.[188]

In 2005 Mr Mackinlay wrote to the Prime Minister's office and received an encouraging reply. It indicated that the Tony Blair was open to the idea of pardons, at a time when Mr Mackinlay felt 'the wind had been taken out of my sails'. During this period, he also taunted the Government with repeated questions about why it had prevaricated in answering the questions asked of it by the Irish government concerning the pardoning of Irish soldiers shot by the Army.

Mr Mackinlay's campaign of presenting bills to parliament to provide pardons for the 306 soldiers continued. In November 2005, as he had done in 2001 and 1994, Mr Mackinlay presented the bill which had as its purpose: 'To provide the granting of pardons to soldiers of the British Empire Forces executed or striking a superior officer; and for connected purposes'.[189]

The bill – which would become the Pardon for Soldiers of the Great War Act 2005 if voted in - allowed the Secretary of State for Defence to order the pardoning of eligible soldiers who were executed for military offences, but also ensure that cases in which there was doubt could be referred to a tribunal to be judged.

The tribunal would consist of up to seven people who had served as judges – between three and five who had sat in the High Court as well as up to two members of the New Zealand and Canada judiciaries. The tribunal would be required to submit a report to the Secretary of State on each case referred to it, as well as a recommendation on what the outcome should be.

If pardons in the individual cases were granted, they would 'have similar effect to a pardon granted in the exercise of Royal Prerogative, be deemed to remove or, as the case may be, nullify any degradations and penalties imposed in connection with the relevant offences'.

There was also a clause ensuring the pardons, if granted, would carry no weight when it came to compensation from the Government, but allowed the Secretary of State to make payments where he deemed it necessary.[190]

The bill was supported by a number of MPs including Chris Bryant, Paul Flynn and Jim Cunningham but was, like its many predecessors, timed out.

## Chapter Nine

The involvement of Irwin Mitchell solicitors was a turning point for the campaign. It began when staff examined the 1998 decision by Dr Reid not to push ahead with the pardons. A first point of contact between the award-winning public law firm and the campaign for pardons was correspondence between John Hipkin and John Dickinson, a solicitor and leading figure in human rights litigation. Mr Dickinson said he made the decision to make contact with campaigners 'because we knew it caused a great deal of distress to a lot of people. We certainly had an individual in this firm who was closely involved, whose relative was one of the individuals involved in the courts martial in the First World War.' Key to proceeding with any attempt for a pardon was to couple legal action with a co-ordinated PR campaign, Mr Dickinson said, and he approached campaigners with a view to begin a High Court case, funded by Legal Aid.

During the case, the subject of reparations was not broached because compensation was not wanted by the family. If it had been something Gertie and Janet wished to pursue, the High Court was not the location to do it anyway. The only remedy available to judges was a quashing of the ministerial decision, to declare it unlawful and the possibility of ordering it to be retaken in a certain way.

The question of money would have been one for MoD officials, or possibly for Members of Parliament if the decision to pardon was to be enshrined in law. There was also an ex gratia fund, now defunct, set aside to compensate victims of miscarriages of justice but whether the family could have been a recipient of a Government pay-out was never explored.

In a bid to keep the issue 'at the forefront of public consciousness', Mr Dickinson asked for five cases that could be used as examples of the unjust treatment of executed soldiers, cases that would excite the sympathy of ordinary people. But most of all, a specific case was required, with the strongest possible facts that could be presented to a court in a bid to quash the judgments handed down in field court martials almost 90 years before. That case was to be Harry Farr's.

Mr Dickinson predicted that if successful in overturning the decision not to pardon the 306 executed soldiers, a judge-led tribunal would then be required to assess each case on its individual merits. It was his belief that though some convictions would stand, many would likely to warrant a pardon because of failures in evidence and in court martial procedure.

Mr Dickinson wrote to Janet Booth in May 2002, asking if her mother Gertie Harris wished to proceed with the case. Crucially, Mrs Harris provided a direct link with one of the executed men and made her a candidate for Legal Aid to enable her to peruse the justice she had been demanding. If no greater link to an executed soldier than a grandchild or even more distant relative could be found, any legal bid was bound to fail because it gave the Government grounds to question the relevance. With Mrs Harris on board, no-one could deny the impact of Harry Farr's execution on her life.

But because any challenge to Dr Reid's judgment had to come within three months of the decision being announced, a new approach was needed. Mr Dickinson decided that the best tactic would be to make a fresh petition to Parliament – this time about the case of Harry Farr only – and then to mount a judicial review if the Ministry of Defence again refused to issue a pardon.

If the judicial review was successful, the implications for the other 305 cases was obvious. Shortly after, Mrs Harris instructed Irwin Mitchell to act on her behalf, to challenge the Ministry of Defence on the grounds that it had not considered the possibility of a conditional pardon in its review.

Such a pardon can be granted even in cases where moral and legal innocence cannot be established. It removes the penalty from the person's name, in effect an act of mercy. Although full or 'free' pardons can only be handed to those who are proven not to be guilty, there is a case for a conditional pardon when it is thought that the guilty party requires protection from the full rigour of the law.

Another ground for argument would be to challenge Dr Reid's assertion that paucity of evidence was a factor in preventing compassion on the Government's part. In courts martial, with the state as the prosecuting authority, an inability to retain evidence of the conviction would not be sufficient to reject the case for pardons, it would be argued.

Later that year, the Legal Services Commission refused to fund a report on Harry Farr by consultant psychologist Stuart Turner, a decision that left Mr Dickinson 'incensed'. However, in early 2003, Dr Turner agreed to carry out the work pro bono and by March he had completed his report. An expert in the field of Post-Traumatic Stress Disorder (PTSD), Dr Turner pointed to Private Farr's two-week spell in hospital in April 1916, and the fact he was admitted without physical injury.

'To have someone in a treatment facility for two weeks with no physical injury would seem to me to point strongly to the presence of a significant psychiatric injury or other psychiatric disorder,' he wrote. Examining the symptoms apparently displayed by the young soldier - disturbance associated with loud noise, avoidance behaviour and fear or panic in the presence of shelling – he concluded they were all hallmarks of PTSD.

Assessing the evidence available, he deemed that Private Farr would have known the consequences of not going back to the trenches. He said: 'The easiest option would probably have been to return and then to seek some other way of escape. 'Perhaps this might have been the cowardly approach.' He then refers to the 'interesting phenomenon' described by Private Farr, of tripping up and not knowing what happened until he found himself in a vehicle under guard.

'This description is consistent with the symptom or process of disassociation,' said Dr Turner. 'This is recognised to occur as a common accompaniment of traumatic stress reactions. It is associated with times of particularly high arousal, panic or fear. Certainly it seems to me that if someone had a diagnosis of PTSD then this would be a situation which may well trigger a dissociative reaction.'

In his final opinion, Dr Turner said: 'It is more likely than not that Private Farr did have a psychiatric disturbance and that this had been treated previously in a dressing station admission. His psychiatric disturbance was associated specifically with loud noises, shellfire and the trenches. The specificity of his problem would strongly point to a diagnosis of Post-Traumatic Stress Disorder. In my opinion, it is more likely than not there was a psychiatric disorder and that the diagnosis was a Post-Traumatic Stress Disorder.'

Dr Turner's decision to give freely of his time and professional knowledge was indicative of the strength of feeling that the campaign and Harry Farr's personal case were arousing.

Mr Dickinson said: 'I think people thought it was an injustice, I think a lot of people just felt those decisions were extremely harsh. And I don't think people were upset or challenged by the fact it was capital offences, I think they looked at the circumstances in which these disciplinary offences occurred and I think they felt it was wrong for people to be executed in those sort of circumstances. I never had anybody who said as such that the death penalty was wrong and that was never part of our argument.'

A petition was sent to the Secretary of State for Defence, Geoff Hoon in October 2003 asking him to consider pardoning Harry Farr. A reply, in the negative, was not received until June the following year, but undeterred Janet and Gertie, with Mr Dickinson's help, re-applied to the MoD in August.

Within just two months it was rejected once again. It had called for a pardon on the grounds that the court martial panel failed to take into account medical evidence of Harry's condition. In general, it pointed to the appalling conditions endured by British troops in the Somme salient after shocking initial losses in July. By September, the ground had turned to mud, the landscape lunar-like.

The nature of the warfare was also referred to, suggesting that the two overwhelming factors in the development of shell-shock – prolonged fighting and heavy bombardments – were evidently present during the battle. But more importantly, the petition argued that the Royal Army Medical Corps was aware of the symptoms of shell-shock by 1916, was discussed by the public, appreciated by serving officers and was even a defence against cowardice at court martial.

It was time to mount the High Court challenge, in a blaze of publicity engineered by a press conference and papers were lodged on November 1. As expected, the first attempt was rebuffed by a single judge, Mr Justice Pitchford, on the grounds that 'there is no reasonable prospect of establishing that the exercise of the Secretary of State's discretion was irrational or unlawful'.

A second administrative application was also filed at the High Court and rejected on the grounds that modern-day medical knowledge should not be applied to historic cases. Yet there is evidence of shell-shock being recognised as early as 1915, with the term being used by Charles S. Myers in his 'A Contribution To The Study Of Shell-Shock', which was printed in the February edition of The Lancet[191].

In the study of three soldier patients, Myers, a captain in the RAMC and before the war a leading figure in the burgeoning field of experimental psychology, found the trio of men in their early- to mid-20s all displayed 'remarkably close' similarities in the symptoms that they displayed. All three men had been adversely affected by explosions caused by enemy artillery shelling their positions – the first was trapped under barbed wire when three shells exploded close by; the second was buried inside a trench when a shell detonated and the third was blown off a 15ft-high pile of bricks, again by a shell.

He concluded that the men – largely uninjured but suffering from temporary blindness and often found crying and with clear disturbances of mind – 'appear to constitute a definite class among others arising from shell-shock. The shells in question appear to have burst with considerable noise, scattering much dust, but this was not attended by the production of odour.

'It is therefore difficult to understand why hearing should be (practically) unaffected, and the disassociated "complex" be confined to the senses of sight, smell and taste (and to memory). The close relation of these cases to those of "hysteria" appears fairly certain.' An application for a hearing was made and granted.

Before this first hearing, the Government released its report made on the 1998 review, detailing its reasons for not granting a pardon. The report pointed to a loss of records, which occurred during Second World War bombing of storage facilities, preventing present-day comparisons of those found guilty of cowardice and similar offences but had their executions commuted, and those who were shot by firing squad.

It also outlined the law under which executions were carried out – the 1914 Army Act. The Act, brought in by Parliament at the start of the war, stated that anyone found guilty of military crimes such as mutiny, sedition or cowardice 'be brought to a more exemplary and speedy punishment than the usual forms of the law will allow'. Importantly, the Act required the same standards of evidence as ordinary criminal law in England, that the guilt of the offender must be proved beyond reasonable doubt. It differentiates between a Field General Courts Martial (FGCM) and a General Courts Martial, the former being convened on active service abroad. Simply put, the FGCM was allowed to use more simple legal procedures because of the pressing need for time to be spent on matters considered more important for the war effort.

The FGCM was also designed for swifter and an exemplary style of justice. It meant the accused could conduct his own defence but had no right to call formal legal counsel. The number of officers who sat in judgment was also reduced when compared with a GCM, but for a death sentence to be passed it had to be agreed unanimously. Only the General Officer Commanding-in-Chief (GOC-in-C) could confirm or commute a death sentence awarded by a FGCM. It was not, the report said, merely a rubber-stamping process because just 11 per cent of death sentences were actually carried out.

The report also looked at the historical context of the executions and points to the fact that men were routinely taken out of the line to recover from the strain of trench warfare, suggesting that the military hierarchy were well aware that soldiers would break down if forced to spend too much time at the front.

Focusing on shell-shock, the report said that understanding of Combat Stress Reaction (CSR) during the First World War was greater than generally realised and it continued to develop during the war. However, there was no standard diagnosis and sympathy and views on the condition varied between medical officers. It shows that 520 men were diagnosed as suffering from 'functional nervous diseases' between August and December 1914. Also, 60,000 men received war pensions after the Armistice as psychiatric cases.

Cases of shell-shock became acute in July 1916 after the start of the Battle of the Somme. Thousands were rendered incapable. To address the problem of shell-shock, special centres were set up in all Army areas to process soldiers claiming to suffer from the condition and as a result the number of shell-shock casualties among infantry fell by 66 per cent in 1917 compared with the previous year.

The suggestion is that in 1916, military authorities had become overwhelmed with soldiers claiming shell-shock, the majority of which were not genuine. This was the background to Harry Farr's trial and execution – a system ill-equipped to deal with men who were suffering in the deteriorating conditions of the Somme, be they psychologically damaged or merely unwilling to continue fighting.

Using this report, the Irwin Mitchell legal team began preparing the case for a pardon on the basis that the sentence and not the conviction was unjust. Legal aid was obtained for QC representation and a further report by Dr Turner, also funded by the Legal Services Commission, effectively rebutted the Government's argument that a diagnosis of Harry Farr's condition could not be made from the present day.

Mr Dickinson said: 'Legal Aid was critical. In all fairness I have my gripes with the Legal Services Commission but they were really good in this case. We went in any event so far over budget in this case that I know my boss was a little twitchy. He answers to the powers that be. But the Commission was very good.'

In December 2004 Julian Knowles, a barrister with the Matrix Chambers, was asked by Mr Dickinson to take the case on after the failure of the application for judicial review. Mr Knowles, an experienced public law, criminal law and human rights lawyer and an expert in field of the death penalty around the world, accepted, being fully aware of the controversy surrounding the case for pardons. He said: 'You don't have to look very far in the literature, this is always used as an example of an obvious miscarriage of justice, even before this case it was generally recognised. Even those who don't support pardons I think would accept that Harry's case was a miscarriage of justice.'

Mr Knowles called on Edward Fitzgerald QC to lead him in the case. The pair were friends and importantly had worked together in death penalty cases in the Privy Council, the London court that provides many of Great Britain's former colonies their highest court of appeal. The challenge for Mr Fitzgerald and Mr Knowles was to find a new way of challenging for a review, after the initial failure.

Mr Knowles' initial advice to his new client, Gertie Harris, was that the decision by the Secretary of State for Defence Geoff Hoon not to grant a pardon to Harry Farr was flawed in at least three ways. Firstly, his decision – sent to the family in a letter on October 19 2004 - was made on the basis of material not seen by the applicants which was unfair. The material related to medical advice given to ministers for the 1998 review of First World War execution cases and Mr Knowles believed the review only examined a small number of cases. The advice suggested that retrospective diagnosis was impossible, something that was contradicted by Dr Turner's 2003 report. The failure to disclose the material that provided the basis of the decision was fundamentally unfair, Mr Knowles said. Secondly, Mr Hoon failed to assess Harry's treatment against modern levels of fairness, meaning he had not properly considered whether either a free or a conditional pardon was possible. The precedent for such approach was set in the appeal case of Derek Bentley (deceased) in 1998. Bentley was the last man to be hanged for murder in Britain despite not firing the fatal shot that killed a policeman in 1952.

A posthumous royal pardon was granted in 1993, but the conviction remained and it was not until a 1998 Court of Appeal judgment that it was quashed. In the judgment, Lord Bingham of Cornhill, the Chief Justice of England, said where there had been significant changes in the standards of fairness between conviction and appeal, modern standards had to be applied, even if they could not have been at the time.

Finally, he failed to give reasons for the refusal. The compelling contemporary evidence from court martial witnesses who described Harry as suffering from shell-shock in 1915 as well as good character references were not addressed by the Secretary of State. Mr Knowles believed such evidence provided the basis for a case for a pardon, yet it was not addressed and as a result told his client that the decision was unlawful and should be quashed.

To do this, a Grounds of Challenge needed to be drafted, and a suitable Queen's Counsel – Mr Fitzgerald - was employed due to the complexity of the case. Mr Fitzgerald QC is a human rights barrister, with expertise in public and criminal law fields such as the death penalty and extradition as well as successful experience in judicial review cases.

Since Harry Farr's case he has been awarded the CBE for services to human rights and has been recognised as Human Rights and Public Law Silk of the Year. Before it he had represented the killer of two-year-old Jamie Bulger, Jon Venables, after then-Home Secretary Michael Howard had increased the minimum tariff imposed upon Venables and his fellow murderer, Robert Thompson, from eight to 15 years.

Mr Fitzgerald's appearances in the European Court of Human Rights led to the overturning of the increase and an end to political intrusion into sentencing in individual cases. He was also involved in the case for a posthumous pardoning of Bentley, the case that was to prove critical to Harry's.

The next step was to request the material that was used as the basis of the decision. Irwin Mitchell sent the request to the Secretary of State and within a few weeks the reports were returned – the first was Dr Martin Deahl's report to the Surgeon General in July 1997.

The report was prepared for the new Labour government's 1998 review of the 306 First World War executions and was entitled The Effects on Combatants and Attitudes to Stress-Related Disorders in the British Army in World War One. The other report was the Ministry of Defence's Review into First World War executions.

The legal team now had a new basis for a case and on May 16 2005 there was a hearing in the High Court before Mr Justice Stanley Burton. The two strands of the case, which was a renewed application for judicial review, were that Harry was not properly medically examined and that Field Marshal Haig was not aware of evidence that could have saved Harry when he confirmed the death sentence.

Simon Wesseley, a Government psychiatrist and later to become the president of the Royal College of Psychiatrists, gave evidence in the case. He did not contradict the assertion that Harry had suffered from shell-shock, but said that deaths such as Harry's were an unfortunate and tragic consequence of war.

Mr Justice Stanley Burton, who was 'remarkably sympathetic', did not consider it possible to establish a diagnosis of shell-shock because of the distance of time and the limited information available. He confirmed that the Ministry of Defence was correct in refusing a full pardon because of the high standard of proof required had not been reached.

However, in terms of a conditional pardon he felt there was an arguable case. The argument put forward on behalf of Gertie was that the wrong test had been applied by Secretary of State. It meant a full hearing on the matter would take place in October and that hearing was to have a huge impact on the MoD because of the media interest in it.

A press release was issued to national press and broadcast media ahead of the October hearing, containing quotes from Gertie, Mr Dickinson and Mr Hipkin. In it, Gertie said: 'Once my father went to France he never returned home on leave. He received treatment for the condition then known as shell-shock, but the court martial didn't take into account the evidence of his illness or his previous good record as a soldier. Instead they convicted and executed him when his company commander described his nerves as "destroyed".'[192]

Photographers gathered outside the famous buildings in The Strand, central London, and the ensuing images of Gertie, surrounded by family including Janet, legal representatives and campaigners were invaluable for piling pressure on Labour ministers.

Prior to the hearing, Mr Knowles and Mr Fitzgerald, firm friends, met in a tapas restaurant in Shepherd's Bush, west London to mull the case over. Mr Knowles was convinced there would be a way to further their argument that hadn't been put forward before and as they pushed the details to and fro, the pair had a moment of enlightenment which Mr Knowles would later describe as 'like something out of a film'.

The barristers considered the test that had been used to judge the case by the MoD - the test established in the appeal court hearing in which relatives of Derek Bentley, the last man to be hanged in Britain, had demanded he be pardoned. The test in that case, brought in 1993, was to see if there was any evidence that allowed the death sentence imposed for murder to be commuted to life imprisonment, enabling a conditional pardon.

The Home Office test had been reapplied by the MoD to Harry's case, which had one crucial difference to that of Bentley, the men came to realise. At the time Bentley was convicted of murder, the death penalty for the offence was mandatory. The ultimate penalty for cowardice, as laid down in the Army Act of 1914, was also execution, but it was not a mandatory penalty.

Referring to the military's non-mandatory death sentence, which was ultimate sanction for a number of offences, Mr Fitzgerald said: 'Because it was discretionary, to apply the test you would apply for mandatory was wrong and once it's discretionary you'd look at all the factors. Which I was aware of because I'd been doing all these test cases on the mandatory death penalty.'

Mr Knowles said: 'If you look at that question and you add in what was known at the time about Harry's case, namely he was shell-shocked, and you add in only five to 10 per cent of people [were actually executed compared to those sentenced to death], the MoD question should have been, on what we know now and what was known at the time, should HF ever have been sentenced to death at all?' Mr Fitzgerald said: 'We were going for the misdirection of law. It came from all the death penalty cases. He [Reid] got that wrong at the MoD.'

Mr Bentley was found guilty of the murder of PC Sidney Miles who was shot dead by his 16-year-old accomplice during a bungled burglary at a warehouse in Croydon, south London. Despite appealing against his conviction, he was executed on January 28 1953 at the age of 19. Though he did not fire the fatal shot, Mr Bentley was convicted of murder, yet his family fought to overturn that conviction, which brought with it a mandatory sentence of death by execution.

Mr Fitzgerald worked on the case to overturn his conviction – a process started by his parents and taken on by his sister after their deaths in the 1970s. On July 30 1998, The Lord Chief Justice of England, Lord Bingham of Cornhill, read out his judgment in the Court of Appeal. Two points were critical to the decision. Firstly, the law of murder as applicable at the time had to be applied to the case, despite important changes as part of the later Homicide Act 1957.

Secondly, the safety of the conviction had to be considered 'according to the standards we would now apply', meaning modern-day standards of justice could be used to influence the decision. For critics, this would demonstrate how the values of today were being used to inform the decisions of the past – the rewriting of history in action.

Today, countries that continue to impose the death penalty in a discretionary manner for murder cases are often required by law to do so only after the defendant has had the opportunity to put forward mitigation. This principle 'reflects an evolving international norm that it is wrong to sentence to death all those convicted of murder and leave it to the mercy stage to decide who should live and who should die'.[193]

Over the years in countries where the death penalty remains a legal sanction (accept in the most repressive regimes), it is held as a most exceptional sentence, for the most extreme types of murder and even then when all efforts of mitigation are exhausted.

In the First World War, the application of the death penalty by the British and Empire armies was also discretionary, meaning a soldier's mitigating circumstances should have been a factor in determining the sentence. In the case of Harry Farr, though mitigation was offered during the trial, it was not considered during the imposition of the sentence. Indeed, Harry's fate was reliant on the unsatisfactory confirmation process, in which increasingly senior officers with scant knowledge of the case except the notes in front of them were tasked with recommending death or mercy.

These were some of the most senior soldiers in the British Army, tasked with fighting a war of unprecedented slaughter and they often received such papers in the middle of offensives.

It would be fair to suggest that cases such as Harry's did not command their undivided attention. This administrative procedure of the application of mercy proved wholly unsuitable in Harry's case because despite being deserving of the commuting of his sentence, he was failed by his military superiors.

Clearly the process worked in the vast majority of cases with 90 per cent of the more than 3,000 death sentences not being carried out after a recommendation of mercy. And yet examination of Harry's case and others among the 306 show that men deserving of mercy were sent to their deaths. It shows a process that was arbitrary at best, and selectively cruel at worst.

The language used by officers in confirming the sentence demonstrate at once how they failed to recognise the need to show mercy in Harry's case and how an element of exemplary justice was at the forefront of at least one of their minds: 'It is not known what destroyed this man's nerves'. And also: 'The men know that this man is no good'.[194]

The inference from the latter is that if the men know a fellow soldier was incapable of assisting them in combat, but was taken away and either discharged or hospitalised, that the cost to morale and discipline would be severe.

The breakthrough meant that points of contention that had dogged the case for years, namely whether it was right to view it through the eyes of modern medicine or judge it by modern standards of fairness could be set aside. Instead at the hearing in October, the judge was presented with the new argument and was impressed.

The MoD barrister objected to the submission of new evidence, appealing to the judge to assess the case on previous evidence. But the judge said the new argument had merit and instructed the Government side to go away and look at its decision again in light of it.

Mr Fitzgerald said: 'We were sitting around that weekend playing with the Bentley test and all that and I remember saying "this is completely wrong, this a discretionary system" because we went back and looked at the whole thing but it was discretionary. We drafted out this thing on the Saturday or the Sunday and served it on the judge on the night before and also the other side.

'That was what touched it. Once he said to the MoD go away and think about it and I remember saying to my opposite number we are going to push on and go for a judgment unless you can tell me, when they say it will be a serious consideration, he said it will be a serious consideration. The minister is committed. Effectively he was saying this won't be just a perfunctory, we've got to do it for the courts, this will be a genuine consideration of the whole issue.'

'I remember Judge Walker basically saying to him (MoD) "you may like what I say about this but you won't like what I say about that". And then he put our new point to him and said if the Secretary of State has started from the wrong premise that it was justly imposed and in fact in a discretionary system it should never have been imposed in the first place, what then?'

Mr Dickinson said: 'After the October hearing the MoD was always on the back foot because Gertie was outside the court supported by all her family and it was very moving, she was saying she didn't want compensation, she just wanted justice for her father. It was quite clear that no-one in the family was in the least bit interested in a compensation claim. They just wanted justice and it was very, very attractive to the media.'

The case was adjourned so the Government could consider the new arguments put forward on Gertie's behalf. Significantly, it had agreed to look again at its original decision not to grant the pardon. The Secretary of State was to consider the matter on the basis that Harry should not have been sentenced to death in a discretionary system because of the presence of shell-shock in his case.

It was also going to be looked at on the basis that there were defects in the sentencing process, compared with previous decisions to maintain the status quo because it was believed that 'due judicial process' had been followed. The submission pointed to other subsequent cases that established the principle that the emergence of doubt surrounding the medical history of the patient should lead to the death penalty not being imposed. One of them was the 1995 South African Constitutional Court decision in the case of quadruple murderer T. Makwanyane, who had been sentenced to death with another man for his crimes.[195] It led to South Africa abandoning the death penalty on the basis that its new constitution upheld the sanctity of human life. Among the argument's conclusions was that the Secretary of State had to accept that Harry had been treated for shell-shock in 1915 and problems with his nerves twice in the year he died.

The evidence at the court martial hearing from an officer who said he was incapable of not panicking suggests he was also suffering from mental problems at the time he committed the military crime of cowardice – casting further doubt on his conviction and subsequent sentence.

Finally, it called on the Secretary of State to apply the proper test regarding shell-shock, as it should have been at the time and indeed as it was in the vast majority of other cases. As a consequence, Gertie and Janet were invited to the Ministry of Defence to meet ministers and discuss the case, a sign that its significance had changed in their eyes. Mr Dickinson said: 'Reid's approach may have been "There may be some wrong decisions made but the majority were OK so we'll leave it". I think the subsequent approach was "it was a long time ago", secondly there is a groundswell of opinion and thirdly a different emphasis, "there were some innocent people there, we can't distinguish so we will pardon all". Which is completely the other way of looking at it.'

Despite the partial successes of the hearing, there were concerns among campaigners that because of Gertie's age, any future MoD heel-dragging could lead to her not seeing the pardons obtained in her lifetime. And equally as worrying, if she had passed away at this stage, Janet would not have been automatically eligible for Legal Aid. However, because of the case's high-profile nature, it would have been incredibly damaging if the Government was seen to de-rail it by underhand means. In reality, if Gertie died, her publicly funded case would simply have passed to Janet.

In December, the Ministry of Defence responded to further petitions filed by Gertie's legal team. At this stage, a critical error was made, one that revealed the Ministry of Defence's utter intransigence on the matter. In the process of disclosing the skeleton argument for Irwin Mitchell and the barristers to scrutinise, the MoD included a letter from the senior civil servant who was handling the case. The letter showed that without even hearing further submissions from the applicant, MoD decision-makers had already decided pardons were not appropriate.

The letter apparently made reference to the fact that the MoD was corresponding with its barrister in a bid to find out how the case could be quickly disposed of and the same decision maintained. Mr Knowles said: 'There was a letter that made it clear that at the time they were promising they were having genuinely open-minded discussions. 'In fact what they were doing was trying to reach the same decision irrespective of what we said, they were determined at all costs to uphold their original decision.'

Mr Dickinson said: 'It further put the MoD on the back foot because we were saying "they go through the consultation procedure and they've already told their legal team that they're not going to accept it". We dealt with that on their argument which was the final argument saying it was all irrelevant, the points they'd made.'

Mr Knowles put this obstinacy down to a perception that pardons would superimpose the values of the present on history. He also believed that civil servants operate with a natural conservatism, looking for reasons not to instigate change. Finally, the family's barrister said a decision to issue a pardon or even a blanket pardon had serious implications for authorities despite the passage of time because it would be an admission of serious wrongdoing. He said: 'If it was ever proper to shoot somebody – some of the cases no doubt were meritorious according to their terms – but there was a reluctance on the part of the civil servants to acknowledge if they had gone along with the pardon, as a consequence of that there were a lot of people who were shot who shouldn't have been shot. Partly a human reaction against that and partly they wanted to preserve the reputation of the Army.'

In February 2006, the case hit the headlines again in the wake of new Defence Secretary Dr Reid's latest decision not to issue pardons in wake of the High Court appeal for him to reconsider. The Observer reported[196] on Dr Reid's decision not to allow an individual pardon for Harry Farr having asked the High Court for more time to consider the case the previous November.

Gertie Harris, then aged 93, said she was disappointed with the decision, which was branded 'horrific' by Shot At Dawn campaigner Mr Hipkin. The report said that MoD lawyers had rejected the High Court bid for a pardon on the grounds that it could not be proven conclusively that shell-shock was behind Harry's refusal to return to the front.

But Mr Dickinson, said he had evidence of the government deeming the dismissal from the Army of an officer for a similar offence as too harsh a punishment when the case was reviewed in 1922. 'Perhaps [it was] because one involves a private and the other an officer', he said. The article was illustrated by the by-now iconic picture of Harry, but the image also showed Janet's hands clasping the photograph, in a reminder of the family's involvement in the case.

On the same day, the political editor of the Sunday Mirror Paul Gilfeather claimed an exclusive[197] stating that the pardons campaign was close to victory because Mr Mackinlay was planning to call for an amendment to a new bill on Army discipline, forcing a vote on the matter. Mr Mackinlay said he had the support of the Commons and the Lords, blaming the MoD and 'generals and other top brass' for resistance to the campaign. As all parties prepared to return to court the following month, the Shot At Dawn campaign's autonomous volunteers were continuing to put pressure on authorities.

Shot At Dawn's efforts to gain access to the Royal Archives had resulted in 'the Queen [being] dragged into the fierce row, the Sunday Mirror reported[198]. The group wanted to prove her grandfather King George V signed 'unfair' pardons for officers because of class prejudice – just two of the 306 executed were officers. Mr Hipkin said: 'It's the old school tie thing – a lot of the officers were from good families and ex-Etonians. There was blatant prejudice about which men would face the firing squad.' In a skeleton argument submitted on March 21 2006, Gertie's legal team formally accused the Government of already making the decision. On March 27 2006, the family of Harry Farr returned to the High Court for the latest hearing in a bid to get Dr Reid to reconsider his decision. The judge, unimpressed by this development, reprimanded the MoD and again told its staff to undertake a proper examination of the arguments put forward. Mr Fitzgerald, for the family, told the court that new evidence had come to light, saying the soldier was probably suffering from what is now known as PTSD. He called on Dr Reid to reconsider the case 'with a genuine open mind and his decision will not be determined on policy grounds'.

After a morning of out-of-court talks, it was announced that Dr Reid would reconsider pardoning Harry, in a move that was heralded as a breakthrough in the campaign when it was reported on the next day by all national newspapers. Jonathan Crow, the First Treasury Counsel acting for the Government, also said Dr Reid was giving 'serious consideration' to a request for a personal meeting with Gertie.

Mr Justice Walker agreed to an adjournment in the case, saying 'effectively the matter starts again afresh'. It meant that the application for judicial review would only continue if Dr Reid again refused a pardon. A number of newspapers, including the Daily Mail, reported on what Gertie wanted to say to Dr Reid. She said: 'I would just like to say, "please give him the pardon, just to prove he was not a coward. He was a very brave soldier who died for his country. He was just ill. He had shell-shock'.[199] The Daily Telegraph reported Gertie as saying that in light of her father spending almost two years on the Western Front, 'I don't think most people could stand a weekend of it, all that death around you. The noise got to him in the end. He was a victim of shell-shock who was never given a fair trial.'[200]

In an editorial piece, the Daily Mirror backed the campaign to pardon Harry. It said: 'Defence Secretary John Reid cannot turn back the clock but he can make some amends by granting a posthumous pardon to Pte Farr and the other troops treated so disgracefully during the First World War. This is not a re-writing of history but acknowledging that innocent men were wronged in that brutal conflict.'[201]

Newspapers continued to carry varied opinions on the matter, and were broadly supportive. A Sunday Mirror columnist reminded readers of the difference in treatment by senior officers of Siegfried Sassoon when compared with what happened to Harry: 'Sassoon also suffered from shellshock, or something similar. He stood up in the trench inviting the Germans to fire, and was shot through the shoulder. He was desperate to face a court martial but the top brass wouldn't have it, sending him to a sanatorium instead.

'[In the cases of ordinary soldiers,] Mercy was seen as a weakness. Good men like Harry Farr died to cover up what Sassoon described as the evil and unjust "political errors and insincerities for which the fighting men have been sacrificed". Dr Reid knows all about sacrificing fighting men for political errors. The time to put this one right is long overdue.'[202]

Some letter writers argued against public money being spent on the case, and called for it to remain 'a matter of interest for medical historians'.[203] The hearing was to be the last one in the case, and the last contact between Gertie, Janet, and their barristers. But although it did not reach a conclusion, Mr Knowles credits it with forcing the hand of the Ministry of Defence.

He said: 'Almost certainly what the court would have ordered was a quashing of the decision and then order that they re-take it. In this case I think the court would also have said – the court does have the power to have the decision to be taken in a particular way, the court could have ordered the executive to grant a pardon, they tend not to do that for various reasons they just leave it to the decision-maker but I think what the court would have said is we are satisfied the initial decision is legally flawed so its quashed, it's for the Ministry of Defence to take a new decision.

'It seems to us in reality there can only be one decision now, to pardon. But we have to leave it to the ministry. But they would have had a very strong steer because the court I think would have said the only real conclusion you can reach is that Harry Farr shouldn't have been sentenced to death but I think that's what they would have said.

'They wouldn't have said anything about the other 305 cases, it would have just have been this one and I think the court would have been careful to say we are not entering into a general debate about whether everybody should get one, it just so happens we have a very good set of records in Harry's case and are there are particularly compelling features which justify a pardon for him. I think Harry would have got his pardon simply because there are the records, it wouldn't have led without political intervention to the 306.'

Since the final hearing, Mr Knowles has stood in some of Britain's highest-profile cases in recent years. In 2007, he acted for the prosecution in the case against the Metropolitan Police over the shooting of innocent Brazilian electrician Jean Charles de Menezes, who was killed by police in the aftermath of the 2005 London bombings.

Between 2010 and 2014 he represented Shrien Dewani, the British citizen sought by South Africa for allegedly murdering his wife while on honeymoon there. In 2011 he took silk, making him a QC. He also represented victims of phone hacking in litigation brought against News International in 2013. His CV and areas of work are varied and prestigious, yet he identifies the Harry Farr case as the one of which he is most proud. He said: 'I've been fortunate enough to do some really interesting cases but this stands out as being one I was my fascinated by and two I'm proudest of.

'Although the case itself never reached a resolution, that it resulted in pardons is the thing I am proudest of in my career and being able to achieve Gertie some measure of satisfaction is something I'm immensely proud of.'

Mr Fitzgerald said he believed that if the MoD had persisted in defending its position, Gertie and Janet's case would have prevailed. He said: 'If you ask yourself were there any other mitigating circumstances, it is hard to say there weren't any.'

On the value of the case, Mr Fitzgerald said: 'I think it was a very worthwhile case. There will always be this debate – what is the point of historical injustices and all that. Putting it on the most simplistic level we as lawyers once we see an injustice and we have a client who is saying plead it we don't ask any questions we just do it. I think there is some symbolic value in putting right historic injustices.

'I think the Bentley thing was important. I think this was important. We are a country founded on the concept of rule of law and I think it's good that when something demonstrably has gone wrong we acknowledge it.'

# Chapter 10

For all the legal work, the hours of research, the court appearances and the press conferences, it was problems in another Government department that would prove fateful for the case. At the beginning of 2006, all was not well at the Home Office. Despite rapid expansion and more money than ever being spent on border policing and immigration control, Home Secretary Charles Clarke was confronted with figures that showed 1,023 foreign criminals had been released from jail with no effort made to deport them.

Worse, the Home Office had lost track of most of these men and women, who included among their number three murderers and nine rapists. Mr Clarke, forced to admit his department had taken their 'eye off the ball', attempted to weather the perfect tabloid storm, but resigned in May. Serial minister Dr John Reid was asked to move from his job as Secretary of State for Defence to the Home Office, leaving Des Browne to leave the Treasury where he was Chief Secretary and replace Dr Reid. When Mr Browne was made Defence Secretary, he inherited the ongoing High Court case brought by Gertie, supported by Janet. Mr Mackinlay said: 'By the time Mr Browne was Secretary of State for Defence the lawyers told him Mrs Harris was going to win. Of course she was going to win because it was a great injustice. It wasn't rocket science, you only had to glance at it.' However, Mr Mackinlay believed it would be enormously difficult for Mr Browne to overturn the decision of a predecessor, particularly one from the same party.

When Mr Browne entered office, the Irish government were continuing to pursue pardons for their soldiers, public opinion was with the campaign and he had previously supported the issue when in opposition.

Coupled with all of that, Mr Browne had experience of conflict resolution, having worked as the Parliamentary Under Secretary for Northern Ireland in the years after the Good Friday Agreement.

Mr Browne entered Parliament in 1997 when Mr MacKinlay was renewing support for his campaign in the form of another Early Day Motion. As a lawyer, he admitted to being wary about signing such documents and did not become in the habit of doing so. However, in a moment of deeply held conviction, it emerged that the new Secretary of State had once signed such a document, opening him to the same accusations of hypocrisy to which Dr Reid had been subjected.

Mr Browne said: 'I was told at a later stage that I signed an EDM and it must have been 1997. I didn't go back and check whether this was true or not but I suspect it was an EDM being renewed by Andrew Mackinlay in the new parliament in 1997 and it was brought to my attention, the arguments brought forward and I signed it in support of it. I was very discriminating about what I did so I would not have signed any EDM unless I was absolutely convinced that I supported it and would continue to support it.'

Now the campaign and the case had a critical ally – one at the heart of Government and in charge of the very department that was stalling and opposing the pardons. Events moved quickly after that, with Mr Browne being briefed on it within days of taking up the office. He said: 'I also came to this with the predisposition towards the resolution of it with some form of pardon so I had already made it clear by my signing the EDM that I felt an injustice had been done, not just to Harry Farr, or to Harry Farr's family as it turned out, his surviving family and extended relatives, but to all the others who had been shot at dawn, that there had been an injustice.'

It was obvious that Mr Browne was serious about the case for pardons when he invited Gertie for a private meeting. He met with her in his office at the MoD alone – without her daughter Janet. Prior to that, Gertie, Janet, Jim and her other daughter Valerie had lunch in the Houses of Parliament with Andrew Mackinlay, his Labour colleague Stephen Pound and Harrow East MP Tony McNulty, Gertie's MP.

Harrow Observer editor Lindsay Coulson was also present along with one of her reporters, Benjamin Parkes. The Harrow Observer had launched its own Pardon for Harry Farr campaign because Gertie was living in the borough. The newspaper, which was to win a local press award for its coverage, carried extensive stories on the case, even going as far as to ensure Gertie was carrying a copy of her local paper when she attended the High Court.

It was clear the newspaper's support had breathed fresh impetus into the campaign locally as Gertie's case continued to move between the High Court and Whitehall. But before Mr Browne entered the MoD, some of the groundwork for pardons had already been prepared by Don Touhig, a junior minister who had responsibility for veterans.

Confronted with the need to address the Irish representations about their 23 executed soldiers, Mr Touhig looked into the history of executions in the First World War and was moved by the case of Harry Farr.

He said: 'It took me 15 minutes to read the hand-written transcript of Harry Farr's court martial and I noted that on the front page Field Marshal Haig had signed the confirmation of death on the front page and yet the space for his signature was on the last page. Now I'm not saying Haig didn't read it, but the man was prosecuting a war. There were 10,000 (court martial cases) altogether of our soldiers who were actually convicted.

'It just occurred to me it took me 15 minutes, did Haig really read it or did he just say death and that was it? It was clear that Harry Farr had not been given any chance to have medical evidence presented, no soldier's friend, no support at all and frankly, it makes me angry still. I was somewhat brassed off with officials who kept on stalling and giving me all sorts of "we must do this and we must think about that" and so on, so I went to see John Reid and I said look, at the end of the day, in my view, there is no more research to be done.

'It's a political decision, either we're going to do it or we are not, to pardon them all. If we are not, let's make a statement to say that, we'll take all the flack and whatever, but in my view we should pardon them and we should prepare legislation to do that.'

Sadly for Mr Touhig within a year of his appointment, he was victim of a Tony Blair reshuffle. After receiving the dreaded DCM phone call – Don't Come Monday – it fell to the new Veterans Minister Tom Watson to continue with the preparations.

Yet the transition between the two men was not to run smoothly, and Mr Watson had to find out for himself what plans were afoot, rather than being properly briefed by an MoD civil servant, a position that was replicated in the case of the new Defence Secretary Mr Brown as well.

Mr Touhig said: 'I believe that the MoD did not want to pardon them, I believe that they were less than honest in not telling the new ministers that they had been instructed by me on behalf of the Secretary of State to prepare legislation.

'But for that call by Tom Watson – perhaps I would have discovered later, I might have asked some questions as a backbencher about what progress had been made on pardoning the Shot At Dawns, because it was so immediate within 48 hours of me leaving office, my successor discovered this that he hadn't been told. Within another day or so the Secretary of State discovered that he hadn't been told about it.

'I think the Ministry of Defence were appalling – they didn't want to do it, there were all sorts of pressures not to do it and they deliberately kept this information from ministers and it was just that phone call that started the whole thing going.' These pathetic, and if challenged, excusable attempts to delay further the preparation of legislation were to prove the final hurdles for the pardons question.

Mr Watson was elected to parliament as an MP in 2001 and in the run-up to the 2005 General Election he was a government whip. At the time he was promoted, he was still in his political infancy and later admitted 'it was quite a big step up for me.' The MP for West Bromwich East said Mr Touhig urged him to continue attempting to allow the pardons during an unofficial briefing between the pair. Mr Watson said: 'The significance of what he said didn't quite dawn on me until I started looking at it in some detail. What he actually meant when he said he couldn't find a way around it was he couldn't find a legal way to do it. When I started to look at it, it struck me as not really the point. Was it the right thing to do? If it was the right thing to do then the state can will it.'

However, Mr Watson was also to experience the collective opposition within the MoD to the idea of pardoning the executed soldiers. Despite being briefed on the matter, he believed he was being pushed down a certain path, away from the possibility of action.

He said: 'I think that the senior officers in the MoD were concerned that if we were to give a comprehensive pardon it would be out of context with the conditions that they were in in the First World War and it would in some way besmirch the characters of those people who took those decisions to execute the Shot At Dawns back then.'

Mr Watson said he believed the military training of officers involved with his part of the ministry meant military discipline was almost sacrosanct to them. He said: 'Their culture made it harder to go a bit beyond the legal framework. It's conservative, it's hierarchical. The military chain of command is everything, authority's everything. It's more used to weathering the storm of public opinion than other departments.'

Mr Watson pointed to the decade before the decision was taken with conflicts in Iraq and Afghanistan as well as the 1998 Strategic Defence Review as reasons why the pardons were not previously prioritised. He said: 'Previous ministers had just realised that it was one of those really thorny medium-order issues that they could easily pass to the next guy doing the job.'

In light of Dr Reid's failure to get the pardons through parliament in 1998, despite previously supporting them, Mr Watson said he believed that as a new minister in a new administration, it was by no means a straight-forward task. He said: 'The Strategic Defence Review would have put a lots of noses out of joint there and a lot of vested interests were being challenged. By the time I got there in 2006 the fallout was still going on.'

Shortly after being made Veterans Minister, Mr Watson visited the National Memorial Arboretum for the first time as part of the 50th anniversary commemorations of the Suez Crisis. He was shown around the Staffordshire site by a military padre who at the end of the tour took him to the Shot At Dawn Memorial where they found one of the 306 posts that was dedicated to Harry Farr.

Eleven years after the visit, an emotional Mr Watson said: 'He took me to one side and showed me Harry's post and it really got to me. I'm sorry, it's getting to me now. I just remember thinking I own a little bit of your history here. We have got to try and put this right.

There was a piece of land that was being nurtured by the families of veterans, they had all got their own little plots, each regiment tended the land differently, it told the story of valour and sacrifice and right in the corner were these guys. So even the military establishment, what I mean is the British establishment, recognised these people needed recognising and it really meant something to me.'

Mr Watson realised he needed to meet Gertie and Janet and invited them to the Palace of Westminster on June 18. He said he was briefed before the meeting and there were a large number of officials involved. Mr Watson said: 'I could tell from the submissions I was receiving that the department was very sensitive about it and there was some trepidation about what we would do. It seemed that everyone was interested in this particular case.'

In the meeting, Mr Watson simply asked Gertie to tell him her story.

He said: 'She told me about the shame that was passed on through generations and I recall her telling me that her mum was in service and it affected the family income and the status of the family in the community.

'And they carried it. This wasn't just Harry, this injustice was passed down through the generations and it affected people's lives for decades after and it was very emotional.

'She just made a very clear case for why this injustice needed to be put right and without judging the people who made the decisions and making sure Harry's name was restored to good order and those people who served their country with great valour but were very seriously ill and had their lives taken away from them.

'I just remember ending the meeting very emotional, I was quite tearful actually and saying something has got to be done here and at this point I could see the officials realising that we had to find a way through it.'

Despite being told to remain neutral by MoD legal advisers, and not to admit liability, Mr Watson turned to his aides when the meeting ended and said: 'We are going to have to sort this out.' Mr Watson's very human reaction to Gertie also extended to her daughter Janet. He said: 'I remember talking to her daughter Janet on the way back to the lift and she said do you have any children, and I remember thinking if she was my mum I would want a pardon for my mum as well.'

For Mr Browne, the answer was simple. Before entering Parliament, he had spent many years practising as a lawyer and serving at the Scottish bar until 1997, mainly in the area of children's law. As a consequence, Mr Browne was inclined to look at the pardons as a question of law, rather than in historical context and narrative.

He said: 'Essentially the difference between me and John Reid was he exhaustively went through all of this from the point of view, I think, of a historian which he is. He was of the view that there was insufficient information to be able to do justice to everybody based on the files, and it was therefore best to leave it alone.

'I took the view that there was enough information to show that some injustices had been done to certain people and that since there was insufficient information to discriminate between the people who were deserving of this horrendous punishment and those who were not, and that we should just pardon them all.'

Whitehall mandarins were informed of his desire to move forward and were forced to seriously examine the possibilities of what lay ahead. Would the MoD be liable for reparations? It seemed as if this had been considered previously and ruled out, in part because of the persistence of campaigners on this point that no money was being sought. Would a new stand-alone bill be required to confirm the pardons under law, or would the controversial step of the Queen using Royal Prerogative have to be taken?

The pardons would eventually be written into another bill, rather that the Government producing a stand-alone act of parliament. Yet still there was concern among MoD officials, some of it increasingly bizarre. Mr Watson said: 'I remember someone saying I don't think the palace would want it and I remember saying are you sure about that?

'I'm sure the palace would want justice for British citizens that were treated inappropriately by the state, particularly those that had been on the front line serving their country and they sort of walked away a little bit. But they were always in the margins these conversations. I could feel institutional trepidation about actually doing it.'

Finally, the will of those with vested interests in ignoring the will of deeply hurt and frustrated people was broken by their elective representatives, a real example of democracy in action. Mr Browne said: 'Clearly there were a group of civil servants who had a responsibility for this area of policy who had consistently advised Ministers of the reasons why it could not be done.

'Whether they were individually opposed to it or they genuinely thought as some historians genuinely do and some members of the military do that it was the wrong thing to do, I wasn't privy to the reasons but clearly there were a group of officials and military people associated with those officials who consistently advised ministers including me and other ministers who worked with me that there were lots of reasons why this could not be done. But I gave the political direction supported by the ministers who were standing with me.'

This support, which came from across the political spectrum and from Tony Blair who was never one to miss a popular cause meant that the Secretary of State had a free hand to play.

Mr Browne said: 'I don't really believe that looked at from here (this point in history) – I'm not condemning the people who made these decisions at the time because I didn't live under that pressure – but looked at from here it is difficult to justify shooting anybody at dawn for this sort of behaviour whether they were ill or not.

'So I didn't feel I was doing injustices and of course those who suggested, historians and others, that you would undermine the whole system of military justice, that re-writing history was a dishonest thing to do, that imposing your views on people who were living under the horns of a dilemma in a whole different environment was a distortion of history, of the world or their legacy.

'They had these concerns but they didn't prove to be true, we went through the process of following the New Zealand model and we applied the pardons and it was some minor response among very conservative historians but actually the majority of senior military officers, the majority of people in the armed forces, the majority of historians and the majority of social commentators said this was the right thing to do.

'It was extremely important that the public opinion was in support of resolving this, it was helpful that there were campaigns in newspapers, it was extremely helpful that the Farr family had the courage and the faith in the right of their cause and the energy to keep this going over a long period of time and to get the lawyers and to instruct the lawyers and be at the forefront of this and bear the constant public examination of the family's position of something which I have no doubt was at least some stage in their family was a mark of shame, but shouldn't have been. The Farr family are owed a great debt of gratitude because we did the right thing eventually and they made an enormous contribution to it.'

Following a question by Mr Mackinlay addressed to Tony Blair at Prime Minister's Questions on June 14, the Labour leader wrote to the MP signalling the government's intent on the matter. Mr Blair said: 'I know that Des Browne shares the great sympathy that I have for the families of those who were executed. He is, as a matter of priority, considering the petition for one soldier, Private Harry Farr, in relation to the on-going judicial review of the decision by the then Secretary of State for Defence not to grant a pardon.

'The review of the Farr papers is being considered in the context of the wider policy on pardons for soldiers executed during the First World War. We understand the urgency that you and others attach to resolving this issue, but I hope that you will agree that it would not be appropriate for me to comment further until Des has made his decision.'

Ruth Mackinlay, Mr Mackinlay's wife and personal secretary, forwarded the letter to Janet, saying: 'Andrew [and I] think this represents a very important and significant step in the campaign.'

The MoD moved towards a Parliamentary conditional pardon, rather than a full pardon which would have quashed their convictions, something that was considered still unachievable for all because of the burden of proof that would have been required. Rumours of a pardon were reported by The Times[204] who said new Defence Secretary was examining the cases in the 'wider context' of evidence that soldiers suffering from shell-shock had avoided either or both the court martial process and execution.

The report reminded readers of Mr Browne's previous stance on the matter, said to be sympathetic towards pardons and a conditional pardon was a possibility, the paper reported. Letters to the paper in the days that followed supported the campaign, with Dr Chris Lamb stating 'the real stain on the honour of this country is the sheer cruelty meted out to these soldiers, even though their records may have been impeccable.'

John Dickinson first became aware of the decision when he received a phone call from a contact inside the MoD on Tuesday August 15 2006. He then spoke to a MoD solicitor, who confirmed the pardons and conveyed the happy news to Gertie and Janet. He said: 'That was one of the better phone calls of my life, telling Gertie. I think it was really worthwhile, it was really important, they were really nice clients. I've had all that combination on many cases before, but in some undefined way it was very special.'

At the time, he described the move as common sense and an acknowledgment that Private Farr was not a coward, but an extremely brave man. [205] He added: 'Having fought for two years practically without respite in the trenches, he was very obviously suffering from a condition we now would have no problem in diagnosing as post-traumatic stress disorder or shell-shock as it was known in 1916.'

For Gertie, now 93, the news was met with feelings of relief. She reacted by saying she was content knowing that her father's memory was intact. 'I have always argued that my father's refusal to rejoin the frontline was in fact the result of shell-shock, and I believe that many other soldiers suffered from this,' she said. 'I hope that others now who had brave relatives who were shot by their own side will now get the pardons they equally deserve.'

The following day, a Wednesday, Mr Browne formally announced that the MoD was pursuing pardons for all 306 men, as a group. On that day, the decision was reported on the front pages of most papers. The Guardian reported that Mr Browne had decided to issue the pardons largely on moral grounds, describing their deaths of the soldiers as a 'grave injustice'.

It added: 'Defence sources said last night that Mr Browne regards all of them victims of the First World War. Whatever the specific legal and historical considerations, it was fundamentally a moral issue which had stigmatised the families involved for more than a generation, he concluded.'[206]

The Telegraph reported Gertie's reaction to the news and she said that she was 'relieved this ordeal is now over'. Describing her father's memory as 'now intact', she added, 'I hope that others who had brave relatives who were shot by their own side will now get the pardons they equally deserve.'[207]

In The Times, Gertie was reported as saying: 'I feel like I am in a dream. In my heart of hearts I did not think I would live to see this day. But I have and I am so happy. We have been at court three times and finally seen justice being done. Harry is looking down on us now saying "it's a fight well fought".'[208]

In a statement, Mr Browne said: 'Although this is a historical matter, I am conscious of how the families of these men feel today. They have had to endure a stigma for decade, that makes this a moral issue too, and having reviewed it, I believe it is appropriate to seek a statutory pardon.'

He said he intended to do this as swiftly as possible, by seeking an amendment to the Armed Forces Bill, giving the 306 a group pardon rather than going through each case and assessing it on its merits.

He added: 'I do not want to second-guess the decisions made by commanders in the field, who were doing their best to apply the rules and standards of the time. But the circumstances were terrible and I believe it is better to acknowledge that injustices were clearly done in some cases, even if we cannot say which – and to acknowledge that all these men were victims of war.'

Mr Watson, who was later to resign as a minister after controversially calling on Prime Minister Tony Blair to stand down, recalled his feeling of joy when he heard the pardons announcement.

Eleven years after the announcement Mr Watson broke down as he spoke of the special moment. He said: 'I saw it on TV. I was on the West Coast of Ireland on a family holiday, I remember my wife just gave me a hug so I got a bit emotional and I am getting emotional now. I didn't feel proud about it but I felt satisfied. I felt more proud for Gertie.'

The reaction to the decision was largely supportive, but The Telegraph reported that Correlli Barnett, a military historian, had described the pardons as pointless. He said: 'For the people of this generation to come along and second-guess decisions taken then is wrong. It was done in a particular historical setting and a particular moral and social climate. It's pointless to give these pardons. What's the use of a posthumous pardon?'[209]

Janet said she was thrilled to have cleared her grandfather's name. The Evening Standard reported that she said: 'He was a brave man who died for his country – not a coward.'[210] Mr Mackinlay was also delighted by the government's decision. The Daily Mail reported that he said: 'The pardons have come through the tenacity of Gertie. I'm delighted for her.'[211]

Mr Dickinson said: 'This rightly acknowledges that Private Farr was not a coward but an extremely brave man. Having fought for two years practically without respite in the trenches, he was very obviously suffering from a condition we now would have no problem in describing as post-traumatic stress disorder; or "shell-shock" as it was known in 1916.'

Campaigner John Hipkin, of Shot At Dawn, turned his eyes to the future, keen to ensure the act of pardoning the men would resonate fully across the country. He said: 'Every year I organise a march to the Cenotaph with relatives of those who were executed, to campaign for them to be pardoned. With today's news, maybe we won't have to do that again.'[212]

Explaining his decision, Mr Browne said the evidence did not exist which prevented the move. He told Radio 4's flagship Today programme: 'I don't want to be in a position of second guessing the commanders in the field who were making decisions. But injustices 'were clearly done', he said, adding: 'We can't be in a situation morally where we cannot redress injustices because we don't have paperwork in relation to an individual case. But we can in other cases where we have some paperwork.'

Opposition to the decision was not vociferous, but concerned the nature of the blanket pardoning. Georg Haig, son of the man who signed Private Farr's death warrant, said some men had to be made example of. The 2nd Earl Haig said: 'It was a terribly sad situation and some of these soldiers were genuinely shell-shocked. But many were rogues, persistent deserters and criminals, or they were guilty of cowardice.'

He added: 'I know my father took enormous trouble to consider the merits of each case before authorising any execution. It wasn't a decision he took lightly. The soldiers all faced awfully grim conditions on these battlefields but some were more stoical than others and fought on bravely. This is history and we should respect the decisions taken by commanders at the time as they knew best.'[213]

For Mr Mackinlay, news of the pardons also came in the form of a phone call, but he was on the other side of the globe visiting Australia on Parliamentary business at the time.

He said: 'I was ever so excited and I remember going to the equivalent of the John Humphreys radio programme in Australia, bearing in mind the Australians hadn't executed anybody.

'Anyway I was on for quite a few minutes, this was a big story. All these things were coming to a head and I think I'd had an indication from the Prime Minister and I heard Gertie was pursuing this. I wasn't expecting news that week, I probably wouldn't have gone to Australia if I had known it was imminent.' Mr Mackinlay believed the submission on the subject by the Irish government, requiring an answer from its British counterparts and still unanswered, also played its part in securing the momentous change in policy.

Two days after the announcement, a report in the Daily Telegraph suggested a 'flood of emotion' had been unleashed across Britain. It said Jill Turner, great niece of executed sergeant Jack Wall who was shot for desertion in France, had spent the day 'weeping and remembering her grandmother, Sgt Wall's sister, who had mourned him... all her life'. She said: 'I have been crying all day. I just wish he had been exonerated, not pardoned.'[214]

The decision had re-opened old debates, the author claimed, about whether to add the names of the executed men to war memorials across the country where relevant. Even on the day of the pardons it was unclear how they were going to proceed. In the Daily Mail, columnist Stephen Glover argued that the re-writing of history was wrong. He said: 'Surely it is an error to apply our own moral values to events that happened nearly 100 years ago.'

However, he praised Harry's 'loyal and loving family', and added: 'for 14 years, his daughter and granddaughter argued passionately that he was a brave man suffering from shell-shock and on Tuesday the Ministry of Defence... agreed.'

The Daily Mirror profiled several prominent cases and featured comment from Dennis Goodwin, founder of the World War One Veterans Association. He said: 'I've never come across a veteran of the Great War who did not wish these men be given pardons, especially those who were in the trenches.'

The Daily Mail also carried a quote from a spokesman for the Royal British Legion who said: 'We fully support the view that these men should be on war memorials. All these people were victims of war who paid the cost of the conflict.'

The Daily Telegraph's defence editor John Keegan wrote an opinion piece criticising the decision to pardon the men, saying 'shot at dawn campaigners were aiming for 'a sanitised version of the past'. He added: 'The Ministry of Defence's decision will have a strange effect on the writing of history since it will not be possible to ignore or obliterate the verdicts even though they no longer stand.'

In a leader article, the Independent examined the difficulties of 'judging the past by modern standards', saying civilian hangings could also be examined as a consequence. However, it pointed to the precedent set by New Zealand, which pardoned five executed soldiers in 2000, and similar decisions made in France and Germany. It concluded: 'This is as much about seeing justice for the surviving relatives of those shot at dawn as it is about rehabilitating the reputations of the soldiers shot themselves. Ninety years is a long time to wait, but the delay does not make these pardons any less welcome.'

In The Guardian on August 19, an interview with Gertie was published in which she recounted the moment she learned of the decision to pardon the men, from her solicitor Mr Dickinson. She said: 'I tell you I think my blood pressure went sky-high. I have high blood pressure and I wonder I didn't pop.'

Recalling her late mother's determination to see the campaign through, she said: 'She was very pleased with what Andrew (Mackinlay) was doing. It was the time when John Major was the prime minister and he said on one occasion when Andrew brought it before parliament, "we cannot rewrite history", and she said "I don't know why he wants to say that because this is something that should never have happened.'

The paper described her as the 'human response' to arguments that the pardons were wrong. She added: 'With Harry, he died with shame and he shouldn't have done because he fought as much as anyone.'

In an interview with the Sunday Times, Janet said she started the campaign for her grandmother, and when she died, continued it for her mother. She said: 'It's been 14 years. It's taken a long time but we can't take all the credit. We had so much help.'

Gertie made it plain that the pardons were enough. Despite suffering financially as a direct result of Harry's execution, she said: 'Right from the beginning, we've always said we don't want compensation. We thought that might be what the government was worried about so we were quite clear about it.'

In the Sunday Times, Harvard history professor Niall Ferguson questioned the 'empty gesture' of the pardons. He said: 'If you are against the death penalty in principle, you may well ask why a few hundred Tommies have been singled out to be pardoned.'

In the News of the World, columnist Nick Ferrari described the pardons as cause for concern despite describing Harry's case as 'appalling'. He added: 'While the relatives of those pardoned are overjoyed, what would it mean to the relatives of those who stood and fought and died if their names were added to the memorials?'

In a political column in the Mail on Sunday, it said for campaigning MP Mr Mackinlay, there would be no such mercy, adding: 'Courageous Mackinlay has often stood up to Blair in the Commons. His reward: permanent exile to the back benches.'

One of the concerns of civil servants had been liability if the soldiers were pardoned. Direct descendants of the victims of the wartime executions were alive and had played their parts in the campaign. Despite some, such as Gertie and Janet, insisting that compensation was not their aim, it was apparently still a possibility.

And just days after the pardons were announced, it was reported that a lawyer acting on behalf of one of the executed men was preparing to put a case to the MoD. Bernard de Maid was a solicitor who had previously attempted to gain a pardon for Ruth Ellis, the last woman to be hanged in Britain in 1955, on behalf of her family. He was instructed by the Naval Association concerning the case of Sub-Lt Edwin Dyett, one of just three officers among the 306 executed soldiers and sailors. After being held under arrest on suspicion of desertion and charged on Boxing Day 1916, with just 20 minutes' notice of the hearing. Believing common sense would prevail, he did not give evidence at his own court martial trial and was found guilty, sentenced to death and shot.

Efforts to reprieve him failed, with a general commenting that a private who had found himself in similar circumstances would likely to have been shot. According to Mr De Maid, this demonstrated that Dyett had been made a scapegoat, symbolic sacrifice made as a gesture towards the ranks, grown bitter at the perceived superior treatment of officers by military authorities.

The attempt at gaining compensation was met with dismay by campaigners and Harry's family. In response, Mr Hipkin said: 'This was never, ever about compensation. This was about dispelling the shame and dishonour wrongly heaped upon these families and restoring their loved-ones' reputation.'

The solicitor appealed to Defence Secretary Mr Browne, making claims for compensation under the terms of the Criminal Justice Act, 1988. However, he appeared not to realise that the pardons would be confirmed as part of the 2006 Armed Forces Act, which was voted through later in the year and did not provide for compensation. The Naval Association's bid was ultimately unsuccessful.

In the Mail on Sunday, columnist Peter Hitchens also reacted against the pardons. He said: 'The excuses made for these men now sound horribly like the excuses trotted out in modern courts... if we accept these excuses we dishonour those who don't make excuses.'

The following week saw publication of a host of letters in national newspapers, the pardons having excited the passions of those on both sides. Some suggested that a blanket pardon allowed less deserving cases to receive mercy, something the correspondents opposed. Others described the plan to legislate for the pardons as 'a rare demonstration of common sense and integrity on the part of a discredited government'.

Some even called for Lord Haig, who signed most of the death warrants, to be stripped of his honours, suggesting it would be possible if pardons were considered to be the right thing to do.

On August 23 in her Daily Express column, Ann Widdecombe, a vocal Christian and former Conservative MP, declared the act of forgiveness in the form of a blanket pardon 'is the lazy and, yes, cowardly way out'. She cited Harry's case as a deserving one but said others were not as troubled as him and less deserving of an official reprieve. The former minister instead called for pardons to be issued on a case-by-case basis.

The following month The Times reported on the work of Professor Simon Wessely, a psychiatrist at King's College of Medicine and a consultant with the British Army. He claimed that the decision to pardon was born out of 'a need to make ourselves feel more comfortable about the past'.

Writing in the journal of the Royal Society of Medicine, he added: 'We can be sure that on the day in question Private Farr was in a state of intense fear, but so were all the other men in his battalion who feared going over the top, as indeed they did the following morning, in an attack in which 150 of 600 were killed or wounded.' He said shell-shock 'was seen as a convenient medical label to avoid duties on both sides of the trenches' and claimed Harry was unlucky because the vast majority of death sentences were commuted.

In November, the 306 soldiers were pardoned after the Armed Forces Act was passed by parliament and received Royal Assent. The number of men did not include those executed solely for murder and the convictions of the 306 were not quashed, which would have been the case with a full pardon.

But the landmark change in law had been achieved under Section 359 of the Act. Defence Secretary Mr Browne said: 'This is not about rewriting history. I do not want to second-guess decisions made by commanders at the time. I believe it is better to acknowledge the injustices were clearly done in some cases, even if we cannot say which, and to acknowledge that all these men were victims of war.'

In a private letter to Gertie Harris, Mr Browne said: 'You and your family will, I hope, now be able to put this sad episode of your lives behind you and draw some comfort from this measure. Execution was not a fate that he deserved. I hope that this pardon can go a long way to lifting the stigma that you have been living with over all these years.'

The Secretary of State enclosed a copy of Harry's pardon document, which he confirmed would be placed with the court martial files held in the National Archive in Kew. The document states: 'The pardon stands as recognition that he was one of many victims of the First World War and that execution was not a fate that he deserved.'

This document records that

## Pte Harry Farr of the 1<sup>st</sup> Battalion of the West Yorkshire Regiment

who was executed for cowardice on
18 October 1916 is pardoned under Section
359 of the Armed Forces Act 2006.

The pardon stands as recognition that he was
one of many victims of the First World War
and that execution was not a fate he deserved.

Secretary of State for Defence

Mr Browne finished his letter by saying: 'It has been a most moving experience for me personally to consider this matter and I hope that it will at last bring closure to you and the many other families who have been affected for so long. You have been most courageous in pursuing your campaign.'

Mr Mackinlay described the passing of legislation as his 'proudest moment' and fittingly, the Act also established a permanent courts martial, 90 years after a field panel decided Harry's fate. The role of Services Complaints Commissioner for the Armed Forces was also established to deal with issues such as bullying in the services.

In December, Ian Hislop, the editor of Private Eye and television personality, wrote about his grandfather's own brush with the possibility of death by firing squad in the First World War. His grandfather, David Hislop, was a sergeant in the Scottish Regiment and during his period of service, punched an officer after being insulted. But his punishment was merely loss of rank, when the striking of a superior was a capital one.

Mr Hislop had previously visited Janet at her home in Farnham when he was recording a programme on the executed soldiers. Janet related to Ian the story of her grandfather's Army service in France in the First World War, his hospitalisation due to shell-shock and his subsequent execution by firing squad.

Of the decision to pardon the 306 who weren't so lucky, he said: 'It was an astute move, since it defused the campaign conducted by their relatives and descendants to posthumously pardon them, without saying the court martials that condemned the men, or the firing parties that shot them, were guilty of any crime.'

He described Harry as a 'hero – but a hero like my grandfather who was pushed too far'. He added: 'There is no doubt, today, that this was a miscarriage of justice and that Farr was a good soldier whose nerves simply gave way.'

For some, the pardons did not go far enough. Mr Putkowski was privately disappointed that full, royal pardons were not achieved. In a pamphlet published in 2014, he said: 'It was… universally apparent that the British government's gesture was miserly compared with the fulsome pardon that had been enacted by the New Zealand government in 2000.

'Nor would the outcome have satisfied Judge Anthony Babington, the author of For The Sake of Example in which he surveyed and expressed informed doubts about the fairness of wartime capital courts martial.

'Rather than a generic pardon, Babington always advocated the establishment of a case-by-case independent judicial review but his opinion could not be solicited because he died in 2004.' He objected to the fact that parliament was 'never granted the opportunity to decide between a generic pardon and a case-by-case review'. However, he said: 'The Minister of Defence, Des Browne, had done well to overcome entrenched institutional opposition by an ad hoc coalition of Conservative politicians, senior academics, retired military officers and sundry Westminster "shadow-warriors".

'Many Shot at Dawn campaigners felt the capital courts martial judgments should have been quashed and executed men's campaign medals ought to have been restored but recognised Browne's achievement and refrained from open criticism.'[215]

For Mr Watson, the recognition made by the passing of the Armed Forces Act was the most significant thing.

He said: 'To have a defence minister at the despatch box in the House of Commons after nearly 100 years, the state recognising that it had got it wrong and it didn't understand all the mental trauma of being on the front line inflicted on service personnel, I thought the symbolism of that was just so powerful. Whether you call it a conditional pardon or whatever, the state deciding that we were going to do it was the key thing. I hope that gave comfort to all the people who were concerned about it.'

Harry Farr's continued presence in the national debate and acts of Remembrance for the First World War show what an iconic figure he has become, because of the appalling circumstances he found himself in at the end of his life.

For a grass-roots, truly national campaign for pardons, the case of Private Farr had become emblematic of the miscarriages of justice that has led to such suffering during the conflict and of the stigma and shame that families felt in the intervening years.

Few people can fail to relate to the plight of Harry, Gertrude and Gertie after he, a volunteer soldier recalled to serve his country, went off to fight in the trenches of Belgium and northern France.

Though details of his exact experiences remain unknown, his battalion diaries reveal the horror and degradation suffered by the men of his unit in those early years of such slaughter. Rarely out of ear-shot of the guns, and rotated regularly into the firing line amid daily death and destruction, Harry broke down repeatedly with nerves. And in the end, he could go no further.

The pardons for all those executed were, after a sustained and honourable campaign led by Mr Mackinlay and Mr Hipkin, the result of High Court action brought on Private Farr's behalf by his family.

Whether or not it was right to execute soldiers was put to one side – some of the finest legal minds in Britain proved to a judge that the MoD had failed to re-consider the case for a pardon properly. Even in death, Private Farr had been failed by British establishment that had decades before ended his life.

However, the judicial review that had been instigated forced Ministry of Defence ministers to take notice, and thankfully they were compassionate men who saw the value of ending the pain of so many families.

Mr Watson, one of those men, held Gertie first and foremost responsible for the success of the campaign for pardons. He said: 'She took on the massed ranks of the British establishment and her cause was great and in the end they recognised her for it. From my point of view she is the person who actually cracked it open because of her dignity and persistence. It was her victory and deservedly so.'

After 14 years of being available for any media interview request, attending events across Britain and unseen correspondence which could have been equated to a full-time job, Harry's daughter and granddaughter could finally rest. Gertie and Janet, alongside so many brilliant and committed people, had won the day.

The haunting image of Harry in his uniform no longer was synonymous with alleged cowardice, injustice and an appalling end to his life, staring down a firing squad. Now Private Farr represented the success of a parliamentary democracy, of campaigning zeal and the sheer love and goodness of a normal family who refused to ever accept no for an answer.

**Afterword**

Gertie Harris, 94 years old and wheelchair-bound, was surrounded by family, friends and well-wishers, attracting the attention of press photographers and camera crews. On a cold, grey afternoon in Wealdstone, north-west London, more than 100 people stood patiently by the town's war memorial for a special service to be conducted by the Bishop of Willesden, Peter Broadbent.

Alongside Gertie, surrounded by her own children and grandchildren was her daughter, Janet. For mother and daughter this moment in February2007 marked the very last chapter of 14 years spent campaigning for momentous change in government policy in a bid to right an injustice that had haunted their family for generations.

After Harry and the other soldiers were posthumously pardoned, Harrow Council, responsible for Wealdstone memorial, agreed to add Harry's name, in a mark of respect for Gertie, who lived in a care home nearby. The ceremony was a result of further pressure by the Harrow Osberver, calling on the local council to honour an earlier pledge to honour Harry.

Reporter James White wrote a series of articles on the planned tribute, culminating in the news just after Christmas 2006 that the ceremony would take place two months later, with the memorial to be updated to include the names of Harry and Driver James Swaine, another pardoned soldier.

Gertie had heard the news of the official pardoning of the men by parliament, after the passing of the Armed Forces Bill in November 2006, while in hospital having suffered a broken hip. Janet told the Harrow Observer: 'The engraving ceremony is what she is really looking forward to. Hopefully it will spur her on to get better.'

On February 20, newspapers across Britain carried the story of the first official commemoration to mark the pardons, held the day before. Gertie told reporters at the ceremony – attended by relatives of both soldiers – was the 'icing on the cake' after the success of the campaign.

The story of James Swaine was also repeated, how he spent 17 months at the front, then failed to return after a spell of home leave. He was arrested, tried for desertion and shot in France on June 9, 1916. His grandson Terry Morrish said he only found out about his grandfather's execution in 1975 when his mother died. He said: 'I was handed papers at the funeral which provided details of my grandfather's execution. It was a family secret and I was completely taken aback by the news.'

Bishop of Willesden, the Rt Rev. Peter Broadbent, led the ceremony in which temporary plaques were unveiled. They were to be replaced by properly engraved names in the summer. He told those in attendance: 'They fought for their country and through no fault of their own suffered vilification and death at the hands of unjust and capricious military tribunals.'

There can be no doubt that the campaign for pardons and its eventual success shaped the latter stages of Gertie Harris' life, affording her a measure of peace leading up to her death. Gertie celebrated her 100th birthday in October 2013, with a party attended by members of her family, friends and nursing home staff. She remained as sharp as ever despite suffering from some frailties due to her age. She attributed her longevity to abstaining from drinking and smoking, but always eating well.On Tuesday February 3 2015, Gertie died aged 101 following a short illness. She passed away in hospital with her daughter Janet and son-in-law Jim by her bedside. The couple had been visiting her at Northwick Park Hospital, north-west London and were in the car park preparing to leave when Gertie's granddaughter Leigh, who was still there called them, asking them to return.

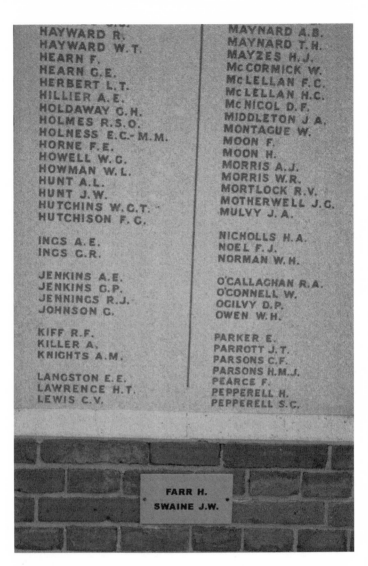

HAYWARD R.
HAYWARD W.T.
HEARN F.
HEARN G.E.
HERBERT L.T.
HILLIER A.E.
HOLDAWAY G.H.
HOLMES R.S.O.
HOLNESS E.C.- M.M.
HORNE F.E.
HOWELL W.G.
HOWMAN W.L.
HUNT A.L.
HUNT J.W.
HUTCHINS W.G.T.
HUTCHISON F.G.

INGS A.E.
INGS G.R.

JENKINS A.E.
JENKINS G.P.
JENNINGS R.J.
JOHNSON G.

KIFF R.F.
KILLER A.
KNIGHTS A.M.

LANGSTON E.E.
LAWRENCE H.T.
LEWIS C.V.

MAYNARD A.B.
MAYNARD T.H.
MAYZES H.J.
McCORMICK W.
McLELLAN F.C.
McLELLAN H.C.
McNICOL D.F.
MIDDLETON J A.
MONTAGUE W.
MOON F.
MOON H.
MORRIS A.J.
MORRIS W.R.
MORTLOCK R.V.
MOTHERWELL J.G.
MULVY J.A.

NICHOLLS H.A.
NOEL F.J.
NORMAN W.H.

O'CALLAGHAN R.A.
O'CONNELL W.
OGILVY D.P.
OWEN W.H.

PARKER E.
PARROTT J.T.
PARSONS C.F.
PARSONS H.M.J.
PEARCE F.
PEPPERELL H.
PEPPERELL S.C.

FARR H.
SWAINE J.W.

At her funeral attended by almost 100 people, a eulogy describing her remarkable life was read out on her daughters' behalf. Mourners were told: 'During the 90s mum was invited to join the Shot At Dawn campaign to obtain posthumous pardons for the executed soldiers of the First World War.

'With the help of a family member they took the MoD to the High Court and after many years of campaigning, a pardon was granted for her father and all the other executed men. This campaign gave her a new lease of life and as Harry Farr's daughter she was asked to unveil a statue at the National Memorial Arboretum. Mum, Valerie and Janet were invited to lunch at House of Commons. There were trips to Remembrance Day parades and many media appearances. In fact she became quite a celebrity in her own right.'

Gertie's ashes were scattered beside a tree in the grounds of West Herts Crematorium, alongside those of her husband Frank and son Brian, whom she outlived.

Her legacy was one of compassion, having achieved pardons in law for those unfortunate souls who were deprived of basic rights, discretion and ultimately their own lives during Britain's deadliest ever war.

**Bibliography**

Babington, Anthony. *For the Sake of Example*. London: Paladin, 1985.

Barker, A.J. *The West Yorkshire Regiment in Famous Regiments Series*. London: Leo Cooper Ltd, 1974.

Bridger, Geoff. *The Battle of Neuve Chapelle*. South Yorkshire: Leo Cooper, 2000.

Corns, Cathryn and Huges-Wilson, John. *Blindfold and Alone*. London: Cassell Military Paperbacks, 2001.

Corrigan, Gordon. *Mud, Blood and Poppycock*. London: Cassell Military Paperbacks, 2003.

Doyle, Peter. *The First World War in 100 Objects*. Gloucestershire: The History Press, 2014.

Emden, Richard van. *The Quick and The Dead – Fallen Soldiers and their Families in the Great War*. London: Bloomsbury Paperbacks, 2012.

Fussell, Paul. *The Great War and Modern Memory*. New York: Oxford University Press, 1975.

Haig, Douglas. *War Diaries and Letters 1914 – 1918*. London: Weidenfeld & Nicolson, 2005.

Hawkins-Dady, Mark (editor) and Charman, Terry (historical consultant). *The First World War A-Z*. London: IWM, 2014.

Hodder-Williams, *Sir Ernest. One Young Man*. London: Hodder and Stoughton Ltd, 1917.

Keegan, John. *The World War First*. London: Hutchinson, 1998.

Putkowski, Julian and Sykes, Julian. *Shot at Dawn: Executions in World War One by Authority of the British Army Act*. London: Leo Cooper, 1998.

Stevenson, David. *1914-1918 The History of the First World War*. London: Penguin, 2004.

Stokesbury, James L. *A Short History of World War I*. Grantham: Robert Hale Ltd, 1981.

Tempest, Captain E. *History of the West Yorkshire Regiment*. Leeds: Henry Walker Ltd, 1941.

Thurtle MP, Ernest. *Shootings At Dawn – The Army Death Penalty at Work*. London: Victoria House Printing Co Ltd, 2007.

Walker, Stephen. *Forgotten Soldiers – The Irishmen Shot at Dawn*. Dublin: Gill & Macmillan Ltd, 2007.

Walsh, Chris. *Cowardice*. New Jersey: Princeton University Press, 2014.

Weintraub, Stanley. *Silent Night*. London: Simon & Schuster, 2001.

Wyrall, Everard. *The West Yorkshire Regiment in the War 1914-1918 Vol 1*. Luton: Andrews UK, 2013.

*A Short History of The West Yorkshire Regiment*, Brompton/Chatham: Gale & Polden Ltd, 1921.

WO95/1618/2. Battalion diary of the First Battalion, West Yorkshire Regiment held at the National Archives in Kew, south-west London.

WO95/1714/1. Battalion diary of the Second Battalion, West Yorkshire Regiment held at the National Archives in Kew, south-west London.

WO71/509 – Harry Farr Court Martial papers held at the National Archives in Kew, south-west London.

## Acknowledgements

**Janet Booth**: I would like to say how grateful I am to my grandmother and mother for their very detailed memories of the past 100 years. Without their stories the Harry Farr Story could not have been told. My thanks also go to my husband Jim for all the chauffeuring he did for me during the many years of the SAD campaign.

**James White**: Thank you to Lottie White for her illustrations, Mike Ward for his work on our website, Sophie Jenkin and John Hayward for their proof-reading and editing and Stuart Emmerson and Gareth James for providing photographs. Most importantly, this is for Sophie, Jake and our bump. You are my inspiration and I want to thank you for all your loving support.

# Footnotes

[1] Interview with Gertrude Batstone (Farr), broadcast on Radio 4's It Is With Great Regret, in September 1993
[2] History of the West Yorkshire Regiment, by Captain E. Tempest, P3
[3] History of the West Yorkshire Regiment, by Captain E. Tempest, p34
[4] 1914-1918, by David Stevenson, p32
[5] http://www.1914-1918.net/reserve.htm
[6] A Short History of The West Yorkshire Regiment, pB
[7] A Short History of The West Yorkshire Regiment, p6
[8] WO-1714-1_1. Battalion diary of the second battalion, West Yorkshire Regiment held at the National Archives in Kew, south west London
[9] The West Yorkshire Regiment in the War 1914-18, by Everard Wyrall, p31
[10] 1914-1918, by David Stevenson, p182
[11] The First World War, by John Keegan, p199
[12] The West Yorkshire Regiment in the War 1914-18, by Everard Wyrall, p31
[13] History of the West Yorkshire Regiment, by Captain E. Tempest, p38
[14] The Great War and Modern Memory, by Paul Fussell, p47
[15] The Great War and Modern Memory, by Paul Fussell, p48
[16] Diary of Acting-Sergeant Walter Watson, courtesy of John William Watson
[17] The West Yorkshire Regiment in the War 1914-18, by Everard Wyrall, p33
[18] The West Yorkshire Regiment in the War 1914-18, by Everard Wyrall, p34
[19] The West Yorkshire Regiment in the War 1914-18, by Everard Wyrall, p33
[20] Silent Night, by Stanley Weintraub, p41-2

[21] Silent Night, by Stanley Weintraub, p154

[22] The First World War in 100 Objects, by Peter Doyle, p121

[23] History of the West Yorkshire Regiment, by Captain E. Tempest, p38

[24] The West Yorkshire Regiment in Famous Regiments Series, by A.J. Barker, p53

[25] The West Yorkshire Regiment in the War 1914-18, by Everard Wyrall, p35

[26] The West Yorkshire Regiment in Famous Regiments Series, by A.J. Barker, p53

[27] The Great War and Modern Memory, by Paul Fussell, p49

[28] http://www.bbc.co.uk/history/interactive/animations/western_front/index_embed.shtml

[29] https://skipperswar.wordpress.com/tag/military-cross/

[30] 1914-1918, by David Stevenson, p157

[31] The Battle of Neuve Chappelle, by Geoff Bridger, p12

[32] The Great War and Modern Memory, by Paul Fussell, p46

[33] 1914-1918, by David Stevenson, p 157

[34] The Battle of Neuve Chappelle, by Geoff Bridger, p21

[35] The West Yorkshire Regiment in the War 1914-18, by Everard Wyrall, p38

[36] The West Yorkshire Regiment in the War 1914-18, by Everard Wyrall, p40

[37] The Battle of Neuve Chappelle, by Geoff Bridger, p28

[38] The Battle of Neuve Chappelle, by Geoff Bridger, p43

[39] Mud, Blood and Poppycock, by Gordon Corrigan, p125

[40] 1914-18, by David Stevenson, p 182

[41] The First World War, by John Keegan, p211

[42] The West Yorkshire Regiment in the War 1914-18, by Everard Wyrall, p48

[43] http://www.cwgc.org/find-war-dead/casualty/399900/ARNOLD,%20ALFRED%20HUNTRISS

[44] The Battle of Neuve Chappelle, by Geoff Bridger, p96

[45] The Battle of Neuve Chappelle, by Geoff Bridger, p100

[46] Douglas Haig War Diaries and Letters 1914 – 1918, p78

[47] Douglas Haig War Diaries and Letters 1914 – 1918, p132

[48] The Battle of Neuve Chappelle, by Geoff Bridger, p108

[49] The West Yorkshire Regiment in the War 1914-18, by Everard Wyrall, p49

[50] A Short History of the West Yorkshire Regiment, p21

[51] Mud, Blood and Poppycock, by Gordon Corrigan, p116

[52] Mud, Blood and Poppycock, by Gordon Corrigan, P116

[53] The Battle of Neuve Chappelle – Geoff Bridger, p109

[54] The First World War, John Keegan, p212

[55] A Short History of World War I, by James L. Stokesbury, p94

[56] The General, Siegfried Sassoon, 1917

[57] The Great War and Modern Memory by Paul Fussell, p43

[58] The Great War and Modern Memory by Paul Fussell, p43-44

[59] The West Yorkshire Regiment in the War 1914-18 by Everard Wyrall, p51

[60] The West Yorkshire Regiment in the War 1914-18 by Everard Wyrall, p51

[61] 1914-1918, by David Stevenson, p212

[62] The West Yorkshire Regiment in the War 1914-18, by Everard Wyrall, p55

[63] A Short History of World War I, by James L. Stokesbury, Robert Hale Ltd, 1981, p96

[64] A Short History of World War I, by James L. Stokesbury, Robert Hale Ltd, 1981, p97

[65] http://jmvh.org/wp-content/uploads/2012/12/A-Contribution-to-the-Study-of-Shellshock.pdf

[66] https://www.kcl.ac.uk/kcmhr/publications/assetfiles/2014/Jones2014e.pdf, p1711

[67] 1914-1918, by David Stevenson, p 208-9

[68] Mud, Blood and Poppycock, by Gordon Corrigan p235

[69] 1914-1918, by David Stevenson, p 209

[70] WO 95/1618/2

[71] For the Sake of Example, by Anthony Babington, p71

[72] The West Yorkshire Regiment in the War 1914-18 by Everard Wyrall p164

[73] The Great War and Modern Memory, by Paul Fussell, p41

[74] http://www.independent.co.uk/news/world/world-history/history-of-the-first-world-war-in-100-moments/a-history-of-the-first-world-war-in-100-moments-a-blast-that-obliterated-10000-germans-9517223.html

[75] In Flanders Fields, by John McCrae

[76] The West Yorkshire Regiment in the War 1914-1918 p190

[77] One Young Man, 1917, Hodder & Stoughton Ltd, London Location 819

[78] One Young Man, 1917, Hodder & Stoughton Ltd, London Location 831

[79]http://www.yorkshireregiment.com/userfiles/File/YREG%20Handbook%20Part%201-72%20dpi.pdf

[80] The First World War, by John Keegan, p317

[81] The West Yorkshire Regiment in the War 1914-18 by Everard Wyrall p263

[82] 1914-1918, by David Stevenson, p 168

[83] 1914-1918, by David Stevenson, p170

[84] A Short History of the West Yorkshire Regiment p23

[85] The First World War, by John Keegan, p318

[86] A Short History of World War I, by James L. Stokesbury, p156; 1914-1918, by David Stevenson, p 168

[87] The West Yorkshire Regiment in the War 1914-18 by Everard Wyrall p268

[88] Mud, Blood and Poppycock by Gordon Corrigan p223

[89] National Archive, Kew – WO71/509

[90] Research by Julian Putkowski carried out in 1992

[91] Mud, Blood and Poppycock by Gordon Corrigan p224

[92] For The Sake Of Example, by Anthony Babington, p72

[93] For The Sake Of Example, by Anthony Babington, p76

[94] For The Sake Of Example, by Anthony Babington, p81

[95] For The Sake Of Example, by Anthony Babington, p111.

[96] Research by Julian Putkowski

[97] Letter, June 8, 1915. Transcribed by Julian Putkowski

[98] Mud, Blood and Poppycock, by Gordon Corrigan – p232

[99] The West Yorkshire Regiment in the War 1914-18 by Everard Wyrall p285

[100] The West Yorkshire Regiment in the War 1914-18 by Everard Wyrall p287

[101] Mud, Blood and Poppycock, by Gordon Corrigan, p232

[102] Douglas Haig War Diaries and Letters 1914 – 1918. Edited by Gary Sheffield and John Bourne. Weidenfeld & Nicolson 2005 p78

[103] Douglas Haig War Diaries and Letters 1914 – 1918, p106

[104] Douglas Haig War Diaries and Letters 1914 – 1918, p244

[105] Cowardice – A Brief History by Chris Walsh, p79

[106] For the Sake of Example, by Anthony Babington, p110

[107] Interview with Gertrude Batstone (Farr), broadcast on Radio 4's It Is With Great Regret, in September 1993

[108] Cowardice – A Brief History by Chris Walsh, p53

[109] The Quick and The Dead – Fallen Soldiers and their Families in the Great War by Richard van Emden, location 3377

[110] For the Sake of Example, Anthony Babington, p84

[111] Radio 4's It Is With Great Regret in September 1993.

[112] http://www.thepeerage.com/p5751.htm#i57506

[113] Blindfold and Alone – British Military Executions in the Great War. p409

[114] Blindfold and Alone – British Military Executions in the Great War. p423

[115] Cowardice – A Brief History by Chris Walsh p10

[116] https://www.kcl.ac.uk/kcmhr/publications/assetfiles/2014/Jones2014e.pdf

[117] Shootings At Dawn – The Army Death Penalty at Work by Ernest Thurtle MP, Victoria House Printing Co Ltd, London, P5-6

[118] Shootings At Dawn – The Army Death Penalty at Work by Ernest Thurtle MP, Victoria House Printing Co Ltd, London, P8

[119] https://www.thegazette.co.uk/London/issue/37340/supplement/5437

[120] The Times, Saturday February 20 1993

[121] The Times, Saturday February 20 1993

[122] https://www.theguardian.com/uk/2005/mar/17/secondworldwar.world

[123] Blindfold and Alone – British Military Executions in the Great War. P261-9

[124] http://www.independent.co.uk/news/people/obituary-lord-houghton-of-sowerby-1345486.html

[125] British Legion notes

[126] The Independent page six, August 16 1993

[127] The Independent page six, August 16 1993

[128] Independent on Sunday, September 19 1993

[129] Daily Mail Article by John Woodcock – no date

[130] The Times, October 20 1993

[131] http://www.parliament.uk/site-information/glossary/ten-minute-rule-bill/

[132] Hansard HC 19 October 1993 vol 230 cc159-61

[133] Pardon for Soldiers of the Great War (No.2) Bill, London: HMSO, November 3 1993

[134] Information provided by the House of Commons Library

[135] https://www.parliament.uk/documents/commons-information-office/l02.pdf

[136] Private Eye – no date

[137] Hansard HC 18 May 1994 vol 243 c815

[138] Blindfold and Alone – British Military Executions in the Great War. P400

[139] Blindfold and Alone – British Military Executions in the Great War. P193

[140] The Times, Saturday September 16, 1995
[141] Hansard HC Dec 13 vol 268 c1033/4
[142] Hansard HC Dec 13 vol 268 c1034
[143] Hansard HC Dec 13 vol 268 c1060-3
[144] Hansard HC Dec 13 vol 268 c1063
[145] Hansard HC Dec 13 vol 268 c1064/5
[146] http://ukpollingreport.co.uk/historical-polls/voting-intention-1992-1997
[147] Hansard HC May 9 vol 277 c 468
[148] Hansard HC May 9 vol 277 c 469
[149] Mud, Blood and Poppycock, p232
[150] Hansard HC May 9 vol 277 c 471
[151] Hansard HC May 9 vol 277 c 472
[152] Hansard HC May 9 vol 277 c 472
[153] Hansard HC May 9 vol 277 c 475
[154] Daily Mail P1, March 16, 1998
[155] Hansard – 24 July 1998. Volume 316, No.214. P1372.
[156] Hansard – 24 July 1998. Volume 316, No.214. P1373.
[157] Hansard – 24 July 1998. Volume 316, No.214. P1374.
[158] http://www.coe.int/en/web/conventions/full-list/-/conventions/treaty/187/signatures
[159] Hansard – 24 July 1998. Volume 316, No.214. P1375-6.
[160] The Guardian, July 25 1998
[161] The Guardian, July 25 1998
[162] The Times, July 30, 1998
[163] Camden New Journal, October 1, 1998
[164] The Observer, October 4, 1998
[165] https://www.theguardian.com/news/2001/apr/07/guardianobituaries.johnezard
[166] http://news.bbc.co.uk/1/hi/uk/209614.stm
[167] The Observer, November 8 1998
[168] The Sunday Post, November 8 1998
[169] http://www.legislation.govt.nz/act/public/2000/0029/latest/whole.html
[170] http://www.nzherald.co.nz/nz/news/article.cfm?c_id=1&objectid=10409821

[171]http://www.nzherald.co.nz/nz/news/article.cfm?c_id=1&objectid=131596

[172]http://www.legislation.govt.nz/act/public/2000/0029/latest/DLM67152.html

[173] https://beta.theglobeandmail.com/news/escaping-the-executioner-one-great-war-soldiers-story/article19895978/?ref=http://www.theglobeandmail.com&

[174] Blindfold and Alone, p299

[175] Daily Mail, November 13 2000

[176] Daily Mirror, November 13 2000

[177] John Hipkin, Shot At Dawn newsletter, March 2000

[178] British Legion Magazine, June/July 1999

[179] The Times, February 4 2000

[180] The Times, March 15 2000

[181] The Times, May 12 2000

[182] John Hipkin, Shot At Dawn newsletter, March 2000

[183] Blindfold and Alone, p294

[184] Blindfold and Alone, p447

[185] Forgotten Soldiers – The Irishmen Shot At Dawn by Stephen Walker p12

[186] Forgotten Soldiers – The Irishmen Shot At Dawn by Stephen Walker p7

[187] Forgotten Soldiers – The Irishmen Shot At Dawn by Stephen Walker p195

[188] Letter to Janet Booth from Alexandra Ward, AD/Corporate Memory, MoD

[189] Bill 87, 54/1: House of Commons Stationary Office, 15th November 2005

Bill 87, 54/1: House of Commons Stationary Office, 15th November 2005, section 5

[190] Bill 87, 54/1: London, The Stationary Office Limited, November 15 2005

[191] The Lancet, February 1915

[192]https://www.irwinmitchell.com/newsandmedia/2005/october/high-court-hearing-for-private-shot-at-dawn-for-cowardice-in-first-world-war

[193] A Guide To Sentencing In Capital Cases by Edward Fitzgerald QC and Keir Starmer QC – The Death Penalty Project Limited, 2007, Holywell Press, Oxford

[194] WO 71/509

[195] http://www.saflii.org/za/cases/ZACC/1995/3.pdf

[196] The Observer, 19 Feb 2006

[197] Sunday Mirror, 19 Feb 2006

[198] Sunday Mirror, 19 March 2006

[199] Daily Mail, 28 March 2006

[200] Daily Telegraph, 28 March 2006

[201] Daily Mirror, 28 March 2006

[202] Sunday Mirror, April 2 2006

[203] The Times, letters, April 11 2006

[204] The Times, June 19 2006

[205] http://www.irwinmitchell.com/newsandmedia/2006/august/victory-for-93-year-old-as-her-father-private-harry-farr-receives-a-pardon-cowardice-and-military-offences also
http://news.bbc.co.uk/1/hi/england/london/4796313.stm

[206] The Guardian, August 16 2006

[207] Daily Telegraph, August 16 2006

[208] The Times, August 16 2006

[209] Daily Telegraph, August 16 2006

[210] Evening Standard, August 16 2006

[211] Daily Mail, August 16 2006

[212] http://news.bbc.co.uk/1/hi/england/tyne/4797655.stm

[213] http://www.dailymail.co.uk/news/article-403609/Haigson-slams-WW1-pardons-move.html#ixzz1G7XBzSa5

[214] Daily Telegraph

[215] Three Uneasy Pieces – Commemoration, Continuity, Celebration by Julian Putkowski, Knowle Hill Publishing, 2014

Made in the USA
Monee, IL
26 February 2020